GETTING TO THE HEART
OF RELATIONSHIPS

To Bo and Tyler
My greatest joys and deepest love

&

To my Mom
Who became my best friend

GETTING TO THE HEART OF RELATIONSHIPS

The MAGIC of Relationships and Their Power to HEAL,
a Guide to Creating Mutually Supportive and Loving Relationships

CARLA PRITCHETT

Getting to the HEART of Relationships: The MAGIC of Relationships and Their Power to HEAL, a Guide to Creating Mutually Supportive and Loving Relationships
Copyright © 2022 by Carla Pritchett

First Edition
978-1-952976-61-2 paperback
978-1-952976-62-9 eBook
978-1-952976-63-6 Hardcover
Library of Congress Control Number: 2022909725

Cover and Interior Design by Ann Aubitz

Published by Kirk House Publishers
1250 E 115th Street
Burnsville, MN 55337
Kirkhousepublishers.com
612-781-2815

TABLE OF CONTENTS

Introduction

Relationships are something we all have to deal with every day. How we deal with these relationships determines the value we find in our lives. Sometimes we are effective in relating to others; other times, however, we seem to hit a wall. This wall prevents us from continuing on in a positive manner with the person with whom we are trying to communicate. We want to stop when we hit this wall and take the time to find out why we can't proceed in a positive way. There is something to be learned at this place of interaction. It's of value for us to let go, step back from the situation, and find out why we fail to communicate or interact in a way that benefits all individuals involved. When we pull back, we want to identify this behavior so the other person can understand what is taking place. Verbally explaining our behavior shows respect for the other person. Respect is something we all deserve and hope to receive. Our goal is to stay focused on our own behavior and what we can do to change and improve it so our interactions with others are more peaceful and effective.

If we want to have positive relationships in our lives, we need to focus on being positive ourselves. We can't receive what we aren't willing to give ourselves. We live our lives and often become so focused on the behavior of those around us that we fail to honestly evaluate our own participation. It's easy to make excuses for ourselves and our behaviors. If we can trust and love ourselves more, we will find it easier to have the courage to be honest when evaluating the part we play in the scenarios that take place. We want to be able to communicate and interact on a mature emotional level.

It's important to be honest and willing to tell the other person what we really think and feel. This is "honest communication." Until we can honestly communicate with each other, we will simply be playing games. These games should be called "hide and seek." We come out for a brief bit of time, allowing ourselves to be seen. We do this when we are comfortable with what's occurring in our lives. Then we hide when something threatens our ability to be accepted by ourselves, or by another. The work is to trust we have value, regardless of what does or doesn't happen to us in life. It's imperative we trust in our value and relate honestly to another person. This honesty is the basis of our relationships. *It starts inside of us.* We need to be honest with ourselves before we can be honest with anyone else. Often, we hide out in the quiet, not wanting to say what we really think, want, or believe because we fear deep inside this other person won't accept us—won't value us for who we really are. Instead, we decide to be someone else to be accepted and loved. We hide out by agreeing to what is said or by giving information we know will be acceptable. Where are we while this occurs? What happens to the person who lives inside your body?

Are you loving and supporting this person? If you aren't taking care of this person, who else will do the job? Maybe you will get someone else to take care of you for a period of time, if you can only convince them you are worth loving, knowing all along that the person you are promoting isn't the real you.

Detach from the love you want from someone else; decide instead to give it to yourself. One step at a time, decide to love and support yourself by being honest in your communications with those around you. Detach from your life a little more and trust you will be fine regardless of what occurs. When we can do this, we will have relationships of great value because they will be honest relationships. They will be relationships in which we actively and honestly participate. We might just as well let the people around us know us for who we really are; eventually, life will let our secret out anyway. You can only live a dishonest life for a short time before it all catches up to you. You will either find yourself in an impossible situation where you won't be able to hide who you really are, or you will die a slow death inside. You will die because no one will really know you for who you are. You can only push yourself down for so long before the anger of not accepting yourself rises within you.

Detach for now. Trust all that occurs. Love yourself. Love your life. Decide you are going to make the best possible life for yourself by being true to the one person you know will always be there for you. That person is you. You are of great value. You don't have to be perfect; you need only be willing to learn.

Relationships can be very complex. It's essential to understand more about ourselves in order to learn and to grow. When we learn and grow, we raise our consciousness to a higher level. The higher the level we achieve, the higher level of communication and interaction we will have with those around us. If you want a perfect relationship, you may have to let go of having one at all.

None of us are perfect. We are all flawed. We all have things to learn. We need to 1) humble ourselves to this knowledge; 2) be willing to start from ground zero; 3) be honest; 4) be willing to share what we really think, want, and feel; and 5) learn to respect and value the thoughts, feelings, and desires another person shares. Frequently, when another person's thoughts, feelings, and desires vary from our own, we tend to think they don't deserve to be respected—that it's our opinion and ideas that are right—so we discredit the information they give us. Their thoughts, feelings, and desires are as right as our own, they are just different. They are suited to that person's life experience. We do everyone a disservice when we discount their feelings because they are different from ours.

Important life lessons:

- Stay detached.
- Trust what occurs in life.
- Take life one step at a time.
- Love and support yourself.
- Be honest in your communications with those around you.
- Take time to listen.
- Be quiet inside so you can hear the truth of the situation.
- Be willing to extend yourself for someone else if the situation requires it, but do it only if it's within your heart to do.

Now you are on your way to creating mutually supportive and loving relationships. Congratulations.

SECTION 1
WHAT CONSTITUTES A
GOOD RELATIONSHIP?

CHAPTER 1
What Is This Thing Called "Relationship"?

What is a relationship? What do we want for ourselves when we are in a relationship? Do we want someone who will always be there for us? Someone who will love us no matter what we say or do? What are our expectations? What do we think we can do to the other person and have it be permissible? These are interesting questions to ponder, and it is important to ask these questions of yourself and the other person. Don't take for granted that you know the answers your partner will give. You might be greatly surprised to hear their view on things. At times we assume we know what our partner thinks and wants. How can this be true? Often we fail to ask our partner important questions because we assume incorrectly that their views on life match our own. It isn't until we hit rough spots within the context of our relationship that we come to find out they may think differently about very important issues.

Ask yourself:

- What do I want to know about my partner? Why don't I ask them? Can I ask them? If not, why not?
- What kind of a relationship do I want?
- How much am I willing to communicate with them?
- What am I willing to risk in my communications?
- Am I afraid that if they really knew how I stood on an issue I would lose them and the love they have for me?
- Am I afraid that if I am honest with them, they will no longer be in my life?

Losing someone is a very legitimate concern, for this can happen when two people can't agree on a common goal for their lives together.

Are you willing to risk your relationship so you can be true to yourself? Not many people are willing to do this. People tend to hide out. They hide in their own silences. They hide behind distractions. They hide from themselves so they won't have to confront the situation. It's time we stop hiding. It's time we start facing our own lives and start to be willing to speak out about what we think, want, and feel. What are you afraid of? What will it cost you to lose the love of the person with whom you are involved? Would you rather deny your personal needs for the benefit of the relationship? If and when you do this, does it strengthen your relationship, or does it weaken it? What do you really want from the life you live?

It's what we want that determines our future. If we aren't happy with our life in this present moment, how do we expect to ever find happiness? Perhaps you are in the midst of a challenge and know that once the challenge is over, life will go back to normal and then you will be happy and content. Why do we keep putting off the things we need for ourselves to learn and to grow? Are we so afraid of change that we are willing to deny ourselves a life we truly want to live?

What is your life like right now? How can you make it better? What can you do to either change your situation, your attitude, or your perception of what you experience? How we choose to perceive our life determines how we experience it. If we perceive it as a drag, we will experience it as a drag. If we perceive it to be a life of challenges with many, many gifts, it will be a life of challenges with many, many gifts. Though you can't change the physical structure of your life with thoughts alone, you can affect the experience of your life by how you choose to perceive it. Be sure to take time to notice the good things. If you focus only on the difficult things, the hard times, that's what you will experience, perceive, and remember about your life.

Choose consciously how you want to *perceive* your life. Choose consciously how you want to *perceive* your relationship. It can either be a special gift or it can be a challenge. Conceivably, it's a little of both. Choose what you want to focus on, then go from there. There might be issues for you and your partner to work out, but it's important to look at the road blocks you put in your path. Sometimes, 1) we limit the potential of our relationship by believing there is none, 2) we give up because it seems like too much work, and 3) we dream of meeting a person who will be easy and rewarding to love. What do we do to help ourselves? Do we pout and moan about our life, or do we get on with living by speaking our truth? In order to speak our truth, it's necessary to get in touch with what we feel about ourselves, our life, and our relationship.

What kind of a relationship do you want? What are you willing to settle for? Do you think you are being too picky? If that's the case, try to be more flexible in who you choose to date. We can become so narrow-minded about who we are willing to allow into our lives that we miss out on relationships we can learn from.

Don't always think of relationships as two people meet, fall in love, and live happily ever after. *Relationships are about two people coming together, learning about themselves and each other, sharing what they have to share, possibly staying together, possibly not.* Be open to all possibilities. Just because you date someone doesn't mean they are a good choice for you as a life partner. They might be someone who needed to come into your life for a short amount of time—someone who came to teach you things, learn from you, then continue on their way.

Relationship questions to ponder:

- Why do we feel we have to love each person we date?
- Why do we put so much pressure on ourselves and our relationships?
- Why can't we enjoy each other more, allow each other the space we need in our lives, then continue on in a healthy way if the other person decides they want to leave.
- Why do we have so many expectations? This puts a great deal of stress and strain on a relationship.
- What if you can relax more, expect a little less, and enjoy the person with whom you spend time?
- Why does everything have to be so serious and so committed before each individual has decided what their needs truly are?

Frequently we rush into relationships because we are afraid if we don't grab who is there, there won't be another chance for us. Why do we think this? Why do we devalue ourselves so much? Possibly your experience has been one of rarely meeting anyone with whom you have something in common. Now you have met someone, so you want to make them yours. What does it mean to "make them yours"? It means to get them to commit to living their life with you. What does this commitment entail? Is it marriage vows, or are you content to live together?

Every person defines commitment differently. One person may commit with their heart and soul, another person may commit for the moment. What does it mean to commit to another person? Does it mean you will stay with them regardless of what occurs in life? How does one make such a commitment when one has no idea what lies ahead? How do you say to another person, one you supposedly love at the time, "I commit to living my life with you regardless of how I come to feel about you? I will stay with you even if I come to dislike you?" How can this be of benefit to both people involved? To what are we committing ourselves? It's of value to look at this issue of commitment. It means many things to different people. To some people, it gives them a sense of security, while others have great fear in trying to commit themselves to something they know so little about. Life can be very challenging. It's wonderful to think there might be a person who will stand by you no matter what occurs. What if that person is there but is of no help at all? What if that person grows abusive with each passing year? What if that person changes how they think, what they want, and how they feel? What do we do then? How do we handle our commitment to love, cherish, and commit ourselves to this other person? What do we do? Do we risk losing ourselves and our respect for all mankind by staying in this type of situation, or do we cut our losses and break our commitment?

What kind of a commitment is it if we can break from our commitment later? What are we really asking ourselves to do when we make a commitment to the one we love? Yes, we love them in this moment, but how do any of us know what the future brings? Yes, we may try to stand by each other's side as much as we possibly can, but life happens and things come along that can tear us apart. Things happen that can change the way we feel about someone. What do we do then? Do we break our commitment, or do we stay with that other person because of the vows of commitment we've made?

Being in a relationship can be difficult. Some of our greatest challenges arise when we are trying to love and to accept someone who is so different from us. At times we might want to throw in the towel, but something stops us from doing that. What stops us? Perhaps it's a feeling we have deep inside. It may be a feeling we have for the other person, or it may be a sense we have that for some reason we should stick with this relationship and make it work. How do you make it work? You work at making it work. You make time for each other. You talk about the things that bother you. You take time to adjust to each other's views and ideas. Possibly the person we are trying to love thinks so differently about things that we have a hard time finding common ground. What if no common ground can be found? When this is the case, we might have to let go and respect each other and our different ideas about the way things are. If we aren't able to let go and offer this other person our respect, our relationship is doomed. *We can't love a person we aren't able to respect.* Respect is part of the package. Have you ever loved someone you didn't respect? Maybe you were drawn to them for a little while, but were you ever really able to have a healthy, truly loving relationship?

What do you respect about your partner? Does this feeling of respect make you feel closer to them? When we respect someone, we are inclined to admire them, which usually does draw us closer. If we lose respect for someone, we are likely to move away. We tend then to want them out of our lives. It's difficult to be around someone for whom you have lost respect. Often, when we've lost respect for a person, we are apt to treat them differently.

What do we do when we lose respect for the person we love? Do we try to tell ourselves we will somehow continue to love them anyway? What are we afraid of losing? Are we afraid this person will leave us? Are we afraid we will lose our house and our financial security? What will it cost us to be truthful with this person about how we feel about them? Are you willing to pay the price? If you're not, what do you have to gain from the situation—and what do you have to lose?

It's not always easy to be honest with how we really feel about our life partner. There may be times when we love and adore them—but also times when we want to be anywhere but around them. What does this say about our relationship? It says that there are challenges and there are rewards.

Ask yourself:

- What do I expect from my relationship? Do I expect only good times? Did I anticipate challenges to work through?
- How much of myself am I willing to give to the relationship?
- Am I willing to communicate honestly?
- Am I willing to work hard to make it through the difficult times?
- Am I willing to commit myself to the relationship?
- What if commitment means to put my heart and my soul into making this relationship work with no guarantees beyond that?
- Why do I need permanence in an impermanent world?
- Why do I think I should be able to commit to something when it's truly beyond my ability to know what the future holds?
- What do I really want from this other person?

Just think if you have two people who truly commit to living their lives in truth and honesty with each other, putting their hearts and souls into making their relationship work; just think about what you have. You have two people who have committed to *themselves* and to the *relationship*. This doesn't mean they will always be together, but they have a better chance of remaining together because the base of their relationship is one of commitment to the *work* of relationship—to the process of loving and learning from each other. The old way of committing to the relationship leaves lots of room for both people to take for granted that the other person will always be there. There seems to be little understanding or emphasis placed on the growth potential of the relationship.

Ask yourself:

- Can I place honesty and personal growth above the security of my relationship?
- Is there security in a relationship that fails to grow with the needs of the two people involved?
- Do I really want to spend the rest of my life with someone just because I committed to doing so in one moment of my life?
- Is it more reasonable to renew the commitment to love and honor myself and the other person by making a contract with them stating that I will remain loyal, faithful, and committed to our relationship for as long as is humanly possible?

We are human after all. Why do we continue to expect so much more from ourselves and from our relationships?

Relationships are vulnerable, honorable institutions. They should be regarded as such. They require nourishment and love. They need to be supported by both individuals involved. How many marriages do you know that do this? Just because you are married to your partner doesn't guarantee you their love and their commitment. How does one commit to a person with whom they no longer wish to share themselves and their life? What do we do when the way we feel about our partner changes? We might choose to stay in the relationship because of the commitment we made to them at one time. We may choose to seek a divorce so we can have yet another opportunity to have a relationship we truly want. What do we really want?

Are we really able to ask another person to commit themselves to loving us for the rest of our lives? Perhaps that other person will, but will it be because of the commitment they made, or will it be simply because they love us?

CHAPTER 2
What Purpose Do Relationships Serve?

What do we gain from our relationships? Why do we want someone to love and someone to love us? We might want another person to love us so we can feel safe in this world. What is our definition of feeling safe? Can another person really make us safe, or is that something we choose to believe because we fear being alone? Decide what you want for yourself. Do you want to live your life in fear of being alone, or do you want to live your life trusting you will have what is most important for you to learn from? Yes, to learn from—we all have things to learn. How many times do you think of your relationship as a *learning tool*?

How do we define the term *relationship*? Relationship can be defined as an opportunity for growth, for further learning about ourselves and about the other person. Unless both people are willing to be involved and use this opportunity for further growth, it will be difficult to continue in your current relationship. Many changes are occurring in the world. Relationships will change as well. In order to keep up with all the changes to come, both people need to be willing to communicate with each other and to be honest in what they share. You will no longer be able to get away with lying and cheating. If you try, you will be unhappy with the outcome. This is a time of commitment—to yourself and to the other person in the relationship. Decide to do this for yourself and for the person you love.

What does commitment mean? It means different things to each person. To one person it might mean you never leave that person's side. To another person it could mean you promise to be faithful—in that you promise not to be physically intimate with another person. What about mental and emotional faithfulness—where are the boundaries there? We have a lot to think about and to communicate to each other. It's important both people involved in a relationship communicate and express their needs about what they want and expect from the relationship—and from the person with whom they are involved. Where do you draw the boundaries around yourself and your involvement with other people? It's quite interesting to find out many people disagree on what should and shouldn't be allowed. It's time to talk about this within the context of your relationship. You'll want to identify your own boundaries first in order to express them in words to another. Hopefully they will be willing to do the same. Trust you can do this. Share this information with each other and you will have a relationship that's more suited to what you want. You will understand the person you are involved with so much more if you can openly discuss these things with them.

It's time to be more open in your communications. Talk about what you think, want, and feel. If you are a person who is used to hiding out from such inner revelations, maybe it's time you have the courage to reveal yourself. Be willing to share this with your partner, be willing to do the work to discover more about who you are, what you want, and the gifts you have to share. We need to trust ourselves and know we are worth loving regardless of what we think, want, and feel. It's only when we can gain this trust in ourselves that we can truly have a relationship that's open, honest, and true. What do you want for yourself? What do you want for the other person? What are you afraid of? Are you willing to put your fears away so you can grow with your present relationship, or are your fears so great you would rather lose the person you love than expose yourself? You make these choices every day. It's how we interact with each other and what we are willing or not willing to share that determines the fate of our relationships. These are relationships not only with the person we love but also with our friends and other family members. What do we share? What do we hide? Why do we find it necessary to hide so much of ourselves? Being true to ourselves is the work of a relationship; to help us heal those parts of us we try so hard to hide. In a relationship, they can't help but be exposed. Once they are, we have a choice—we can choose to love ourselves, or we can abandon ourselves and decide we are no longer worth loving. What do you want to choose? Remember, you are the one choosing.

Be patient with yourself. This work is difficult at times. It's hard to continually allow yourself to be vulnerable with another person who knows you so well—or who possibly doesn't know you at all. Allow yourself this opportunity for growth, for love, and for all the benefits that come from this union. Be patient with your partner; remember to support them as best you can when they are being vulnerable to you. By doing this, we will encourage each other to open up and to share what we truly feel. There is so much potential in each relationship we have. It's the two people involved who decide how far that relationship will go. One person may be willing to bare their soul, but unless the other person is willing to stay present and actively participate, there's truly nothing left to share with each other. How can you have a loving, committed relationship unless you are willing to do the work it takes to have one? They don't just happen, contrary to what some people would like to believe. When they do happen, it's because two very committed people are doing a great deal of work on themselves and with each other.

Commit. Do this work. Trust yourself. Trust you are worth loving. You can have a relationship of great beauty, great love, and great commitment. It all starts with you and what you are willing and able to share.

CHAPTER 3

Relationships as Tools for Growth and Awareness

I f you can learn how to use your relationship as a vehicle for growth, both people involved will learn a great deal. It's imperative that when you attempt to do this, you make a pact to totally support each other no matter what you feel. This might sound impossible to do, but it isn't. The more you can love and support yourself, the more you will be able to love and support your partner, regardless of the situation or the emotions involved.

Begin to pay attention to the relationship you have. How do you treat each other? Are you kind, loving, and compassionate? These are essential ingredients in order to have a relationship built on love and trust. Separate yourself from what you know and want from your relationship at present. Begin to look at it in a more scientific manner. In order to do this, it's necessary to detach more from what occurs within the context of the relationship. It's also important to learn how to really listen to what your partner has to say to you. We can misjudge our partner's statements because we have issues around what they are sharing. We need to learn to let go of our issues more. In order to do this, it's necessary to become aware of what our issues are. Once we have this awareness, we can detach more from what takes place. It's important to 1) stand back and listen, 2) hear every word our partner says, 3) think about what this all means to them, 4) stop putting our own ideas and judgments on things, and 5) relax a bit more, lighten up and consciously choose our response.

Once we can listen, we will hear what our partner truly says to us, not what we perceive them to be saying. Once we can hear this, we will be able to solve a lot of the difficulties that arise—with very little drama and overreacting, which causes stress and strain on our relationships.

We can:

- Learn to come together with our partner.
- Learn that what affects them affects us as well.
- Be willing to help them heal the parts of themselves that need healing.
- Be aware that we also have issues to heal.

Can you be kind and compassionate with your partner as they struggle to release the pain they hold inside? Can you be kind and patient with yourself? A partnership with the one you love is a beautiful environment where you can learn to love yourself and each other even more. It's this love we need to bring into the world. To bring this love forth requires us to humble ourselves to learning the life lessons before us. The more we can do this consciously, and in loving support of ourselves and our partner, the better our lives and the stronger our relationships will be as a result of all the work we are doing.

It's time to commit yourself to a life of growth and learning—and to loving someone as deeply as you've come to love yourself. Be a partner to this person you love. Allow yourself to be honest and vulnerable with them. It's one's ability to be vulnerable with another that will determine the depth of commitment the relationship can make.

Decide to commit yourself on the *heart* level. Decide that your growth and your love is above all else. Do you want a relationship that's beyond anything you ever imagined, or do you want to continue living in your sheltered cocoon? Some may choose the cocoon, but that's only because they don't know the freedom and love that exists in a relationship built on a commitment that comes from the deepest level of one's ability to be present in love for another and for oneself at the same time.

Help each other see what is taking place. Love and support each other through this process. Allow yourself to be known.

CHAPTER 4
Where Does Love Come From?

Does it come from our hearts? Does it come from our minds? It comes from both of these places. Our hearts are where our feelings lie. When we feel something and it comes from our heart, we are unable to detach from these feelings. When we feel something and it comes from our mind, we can detach and get on with our life. Why is one different from another? How can someone love you from their mind? We all love in different ways. Some of us are in touch with what we feel, and we honor it by the way we choose to live our lives. Others may know what they feel, but they choose to live their life from their mind. Which way do you want to live your life—from your heart or from your mind?

How do you love another person from your mind? You think about them, and you want them to be with you. Does that mean you love them? Possibly, but some people confuse *wanting* with love. They think because they want someone in their life, they must love them. This conclusion isn't necessarily true.

Perhaps you have met someone who you think is special. How do you know if they are the right person for you? Can you tell yourself the real reasons why you love them? Why do you care whether this person is in your life? What do you have to share with them? What do they bring to your life? Be honest with yourself if you really want to determine whether your connection with them is truly from the heart or from the mind. Often, we convince ourselves that we love another person because we can't stand the thought of being alone any longer. Really pay attention to what your true motives are for wanting this person in your life. Before you commit yourself to being in a relationship with them, you might also ask them why they want you in their life. By sharing this information with each other, you will have greater clarity about why your relationship exists at all.

Yes, there is love that comes from your heart and connects you with another person. Sometimes this love is enough to make a relationship work, other times it's not. Just because you are drawn to someone doesn't mean they are a good match for you. Stay awake and aware, paying attention to every word spoken. Allow yourself to see this person for who they really are. Also, work at being yourself. Don't present an image that isn't a true representation of who you really are. If you do this, you are starting and building your relationship on false information. This type of deception isn't fair to either person. Sure, it will be challenging at first to say things someone you greatly care for may not want to hear, but what are you going to do, wait until you are more firmly implanted in their life before you spring the surprise of who you really are? Our work is to be true to ourselves. This doesn't mean we think only of ourselves, but it means we are honest with each other about what we think, want, and feel. How do we ever hope to know each other if we want to skip this crucial step? Our work is to be honest and practice hearing what the other person is really saying. Frequently, we don't want to hear what another person says because it jeopardizes the image we have of them. Their behavior may not be what we want it to be. Are we going to face the fact that they might not be the person we'd like them to be? Or are we going to continue on in our fantasy, denying who they really are? Yes, in relationships, people come to know each other and then are surprised to find out who they have really chosen to love. Why is it such a surprise? Was their behavior so hidden prior to this time, or did it just take you this long to be honest with yourself?

Relationships are complex. It makes it that much more challenging because at times we aren't willing to be honest with the other person about who we really are, and we aren't willing to really see them for who they are.

Ask yourself:

- Why do I want an idealized version of a love mate?
- Is it because I want to believe there is someone who is perfectly suited for me?
- Do I believe if I were to find this perfect person, then love would come easily? I would be loved for who I am, and they would be so worth loving themselves.
- What do I want? Is it possible?
- What am I willing and able to do to create an honest relationship?
- Is that even what I want?
- Do my fears of being known for who I really am interfere with achieving this goal?
- What am I willing to give and to share?

- What am I willing to settle for in the way of allowing another into my life? Who will I let in? For how long will I allow them in my life?
- If I ask them to go, what are the reasons why I am choosing to do this?
- Is anyone perfect enough for me?
- What do I think I deserve in terms of a partner or mate?
- What do I dream of?
- What is the reality of my situation?

Give yourself time. It takes time to get in touch with the truth that lies within you. It takes time to allow yourself to hear this truth, to face this new reality. Take time, be patient, and be kind.

What About the Love We Have for Ourselves?

Why is there the perception that if we are loved by another first, then we are worth loving? Why aren't we worth loving just because we exist? Is love something that needs to be earned? Why do we think love must be earned? Perhaps as a child you were shown love only when you did the right thing. You were supported only when you won the approval of the person from whom you were seeking love.

Ask yourself:

- Why do I think it's necessary to win the approval of the person I want to love me?
- Do I not believe I am worth loving for merely being who I am?
- Do I have behaviors that in the past have caused me great difficulty?
- Am I going to change my way of interacting in the world, or am I going to choose not to learn from my past experiences?

- Why would I insist on not changing these behaviors?

To look at all aspects of being in a relationship requires us to look at our own behaviors, and to look at what we are willing to share and to show the person with whom we are involved. We can become so attached to hiding out in a relationship that we forget what it's like to be honest and true to ourselves. For some reason, we have become thoroughly convinced that if the other person knew us for who we really are, they would have nothing to do with us. Maybe they would be bored and walk away.

Things to ponder;

- What do I want from this other person?
- Do I want their approval?
- Do I want them to love me beyond anyone else?
- What do I think I will receive from them if I'm not honest in who I am and what I share?
- Do I really want to impress this person only to find out later that they really don't like the person I have become?
- What am I willing to do to try to get them to love me?
- What am I willing to do for myself so I can move forth in life from a place of love and honor within?

These are important questions; they will determine the course your life will take. The most important question is: who is most important to you in your life? Is it your inner-quest for knowledge and truth, or is it the other person in your life? *Do you love and honor yourself* and then move out from there, or do you *sacrifice* yourself for the love and approval of this other person? If you can start making conscious choices about this matter, it will make a significant difference in your life. It will allow you to come from a place of love and honor within, instead of letting your true inner self go and becoming whatever you think that other person wants you to be. Where is the truth and honesty when you fail to honor your real self?

Why is it important we learn to love and honor ourselves? It's only when we can love and honor ourselves that we will have the strength and the courage to live a life we want and deserve. What do you truly want for yourself? You may think it is to hide out and be true to only the aspects of yourself that you like and accept, but it's hard to love yourself fully when you won't even acknowledge the truth of who you are. Why are we so threatened by any changes we might need to make? Why do we think we have to be so acceptable, so perfect to be accepted by another? Why do we want to live a life that isn't true to who we really are? Why do we think we aren't worth loving unless we try to hide these parts of ourselves?

Start taking good care of yourself. You do this by making wise choices, choices that will take your life in a direction that you really want to go. Don't hold on to a relationship just so you will have someone there. Be prepared to venture out on your own for a while. Take time to get to know you. Be aware of what you like and enjoy. Take time to share this with others. Make your life as good as it can possibly be. Once you can do these things for yourself, your expectations within a relationship will change. You will no longer depend on the other person in your life for all you want and need; you will instead depend more upon yourself. Depending upon yourself is where the responsibility should lie, not upon another person's shoulders.

Be happy right now. It's not the other person who fulfills your life; it's you and your ability to be present in love for yourself. The sooner we realize this, the fuller our lives will be.

Have a good, kind, loving relationship with yourself. When you can do this, you will have a great deal to share with everyone who comes into your life. You won't be dependent on another's presence to be happy; you will be dependent on your own ability to be true to yourself.

CHAPTER 5

Strong, Solid Relationships Begin with a Friendship

B egin to consciously listen to what another person has to say, and regard that information as *their truth*. Give it the same respect you give to your own truth. When you can extend this level of respect, you will develop friendships with others that you might otherwise not be able to have. A bond is established between two people that respect each other's thoughts and ideas. These thoughts and ideas don't have to match, but *it's imperative they are respected.*

What do you want in a friendship? That's where all good, strong, solid relationships begin; with a friendship. If you aren't friends and you are in a relationship, on what do you base your relationship? This might be an interesting question to answer if you are willing to be honest with yourself.

Ask yourself:

- What do I want from a relationship?
- Do I want to be friends with this person?
- What does it mean to be friends?
- Are my expectations different for friends than for lovers?

Look at this information and decide what you want for yourself. If you have a lover you don't consider to be your friend, what are you gaining from the relationship? And is it enough for you? Are you willing to settle for this? Or do you possibly want more? Attempting to be a good friend could get you more.

What Does It Mean to Be Friends?

It means to care about each other, to reach out and be there for each other even when times are difficult. What do we want from our friends? Are we willing to be there for them in the same way? Do things always have to be in balance in a friendship, or do we tend to cut our friends extra slack? At times, we would like our friends to be a certain way, but when they're not, how do we deal with that? Do we respect them for who they are, or do we try to change them? What do you really want from them other than good company and companionship? Nothing much? Why is it then that we expect so much more from our friends when we become intimately involved with them?

What happens to our friendships when romance becomes a part of the relationship? Do we then expect this person to be the romantic partner we've always dreamed about? This could be part of the difficulty. Do we expect them to do more for us than we have to do for them, to prove how much they care? Do we find it difficult to maintain a friendship within the setting of a romance? It could be you are the exception to the rule and have been able to make this transition with ease. What did you have to go through in order to do this? Possibly a great deal of letting go?

When one becomes intimately involved with a person who has up until this time been "only a friend," it's time to release some of your expectations of this person. For some reason, we seem to hold a great many expectations for someone we are intimately involved with that we don't expect from our "mere friends."

- What is the difference between a "mere friend" and a love relationship based on friendship? Should there be a difference? Are we more willing to go out of our way for our "mere friends" than we are for our love relationships? Must our lover/friend prove something to us that we don't expect from our friends? Do we expect and want our lover/friend to prove to us time and again how important we are to them, how much they need us in their lives, and how essential we are to their well-being?

- Why do we want and need all of this? Possibly because we aren't secure enough in our ability to be worth loving so we search for proof from this other person. Without this proof, we are convinced they don't care enough about us—that we really don't matter.

- Is that how you really feel about yourself? Do you constantly need to be reassured along the way? If you do, you might look at the reasons why. Why not focus instead on being a friend and letting go of your drive to have your insecurities reinforced by another?

- What do you want from this other person? 1) Do you want time and attention? 2) Do you want money and influence? 3) Do you want position and power? What do they have that you want from them? Maybe it's not that simple—that there's more to it under the surface. What lies under the surface that you want this person to take care of for you?

- Could it be the child within you that you have been so challenged to care for yourself? What does this all mean? We seek out the company of another for many reasons. At times, it's merely for the friendship they have to offer, but there are other needs we have that aren't so easy to identify. To gain clarity, look within. Ask yourself, what do I want from this person? What do I expect? If you can be honest with yourself, you will discover so much about yourself and about the relationships you bring into your life.

How do we create a relationship based on friendship, love, and intimacy? 1) By being true to yourself, 2) by being honest with the other person, and 3) by being willing to risk the relationship for what you value. It takes courage to be so totally true to yourself, but it's the only way you will be able to have a relationship that will love and nurture both yourself and the other person. Your foundation is to love and nurture yourself first, then the other person will do the same. But until you can do it for yourself, there's little hope another will do it for you.

Be true to yourself. Be clear and open about what you think, feel, and want. Concentrate on your relationship being that of good friends. Treat this person as you would a good friend. Stop the games and stop the manipulations. You can't make another person love you, so don't even try. Be yourself and all that's important for you to experience will be there.

When we can be our own best friend first, it gives us a solid base on which to reach out and be best friends with another in our life.

SECTION 2
SELF AWARENESS AND HONEST COMMUNICATION

CHAPTER 6
What We Feel Inside Affects Our Treatment of Others

Relationships...what do we expect from the relationships in our lives? Do we expect them to make us happy? When they don't, what do we do then? Pay attention to how you treat the other person in the relationship.

Ask yourself:

- Do I highly respect them, or do I barely tolerate their presence?
- Why do I feel the way I do about them?
- How do I feel about myself?
- Do I transfer the frustration and dislike I have for myself to this other person, or do I own my own feelings and reach out to them for the help I need?

It can be enlightening when we focus our awareness on what we feel and how that affects our treatment of the people around us. We don't want to treat people poorly because we are unhappy with ourselves, do we? Wouldn't you rather identify your feelings, detach a bit from them, and interact with others on a more intimate and personal basis?

How You Treat Others

Relationships are delicate. What we say to each other and how we treat each other matters. It's of benefit to everyone if we can pay attention to what we say or do to another person. This may seem overwhelming at first, but just take one day at a time, one moment at a time, and pay careful attention to everything you do or say to another. Awareness to this extent is critical because it's how you build and create your life. *How you treat others is the way you yourself will be treated.* If you interact with others from a place of love and caring, that's what the world will reflect back to you. If you come from a place of anger and frustration, that too will come back to you. It's of value to realize the effect of our own behavior in the world.

Identifying Your Problem Areas

How do we do this? One step at a time. First, you want *to learn* to identify your problem areas. When do you begin to lose your patience? When do you begin to strike out at those around you? Pay attention. At this time, you might not be able to answer these questions. It could take time for you to find yourself in a situation where you are acting out your behaviors before you can say to yourself, "Yes, I'm doing it...this is what it means." Take time then to detach from the situation, your behavior, and your participation in what's occurring.

Stand back and watch what's happening:

- What are you choosing to do?
- How are you choosing to treat the people around you?
- Are you pushing them away from you? If so, why?
- How can you stop right now and let go of what's occurring?

You can call it by its name. You can identify what's happening. You might say something like, "I see this happening and I don't know what to do. I don't know how to behave differently, but I want to learn." What would happen if you did this? You would stop the interaction that's taking place. You would give everyone a moment to disconnect and look at what's happening. You would be stopping a scene that would otherwise unroll unchecked, perhaps into an outcome that wouldn't be beneficial to anyone.

It's important you want to stop what is happening. The only way you can do that is by stopping yourself. This won't work if you are doing it just to control the situation. Your intentions must be only to change your behavior. You are asking for an opportunity to stop repeating a pattern you may have unconsciously developed. To do this takes a lot of strength and perseverance. Ideally, you can work on this not only with yourself, but also with your partner. If your partner isn't willing to cooperate in this process of awareness and change, it will be rather difficult because you will find yourself pulled back into the same patterns of communication.

Effective communication is about 1) *changing* the way we relate to each other, 2) *getting in touch* with what we feel, and 3) *sharing* with each other what we feel happening within ourselves. It's necessary to be able to trust the other person with our feelings. If we can't, we won't be able to do this work in a way that will be beneficial to both people involved. Can I work on this alone? Yes, you can work on this alone. It will be more difficult to do on your own, but it's possible to change your behavior, and that in itself will affect a change within the relationship. However, the other person could feel threatened by this change and might do whatever he/she can to draw you back into your old ways of communicating, your old ways of relating to each other.

It's difficult for some people to let go of the comfort of the past, and they can feel threatened by new ideas and new ways of doing things. They might not want to participate because they could feel a sense of helplessness to not be in control and to not be fully comfortable with what's happening to them. We have to learn to let go of our need to control a situation or another person, place, or thing. What lies before us are opportunities to learn more about ourselves and about the people we love. Be open to doing things differently and you will see the rewards in your life and your relationships.

Believing If YOU Like It, They Will Too

Look at each person in your life and think about what you want from them. What do you feel you give in return? It's interesting that sometimes what we give to another person is something we greatly value and thus think they want. In truth, it may not be something they want at all. Instead, they want something else, but it's something we don't value, so we don't consider it important and aren't willing to put the time and effort into giving it to them. In other words, we tend to give others what we want for ourselves—and they do the same to us. There would be no difficulty if what we wanted was the same thing, but most often it's not. That's where the difficulty lies.

One person in the relationship says, "I want bananas, I love bananas, if only I could have bananas, I would be so happy." The other person says, "Bananas, who would want bananas. I love oranges, so I'm going to give oranges to this person I love. Oranges are much better." It's not even a case of us not hearing the other person tell us what they want. It's a case of us insisting their desires aren't important because we can't understand them within ourselves. Regardless of whether we understand why they want what they want, we need to learn to listen to their words, to acknowledge what they say or ask for, and in return to honor their requests.

Honoring Yourself and Honoring Others' Requests

We honor their requests not because it's something we also think is great but because we acknowledge they are individuals in their own right and their desires might differ from our own. What they think is most wonderful might not be what we think is most wonderful, but that doesn't change it from being most wonderful to them.

To meet another's needs or requests is a great idea as long as you are doing so from your heart. Don't do it out of anger and resentment. This won't help your relationship; it will only harm it. When we do things we don't want to do, we tend to hold it against the other person. Building up resentment isn't a healthy way to live—or to build a relationship you want. Above all else, *be true to yourself.* If someone asks you to do something you don't agree with, or feel comfortable doing, you do have the right to say no. Draw your own boundaries. Learn how to take care of yourself within the structure of a relationship. It's only by honoring yourself that you will ever be able to honor another. This doesn't mean you can be selfish and self-centered. That isn't what honoring yourself is about.

Honoring yourself is about being in alignment with your greater self, or your higher self. When you are in alignment with the part of you that knows more than you could possibly know from your human standpoint, you work for the benefit of all involved. Initially, this could be a little challenging to understand, but once you do the work of honoring yourself, being true to what you think and believe, you will see the effect on the outcome of the situations in which you are involved. You will see the miracle of how things seem to fall into place and work out for everyone's benefit.

It's time for us to begin to do this work of inner-listening and communicating with each other about what we feel, want, and need. Once we can do this, we will find our relationships deepen and our commitment to truth increase. We will no longer tell each other lies. We will no longer want to live this way. Once we begin to face ourselves more squarely, we will be able to learn to live with what we see. Once we can do this, and know it has nothing to do with our value, we will be able to work alone or with others to slowly discard the tendencies and behaviors we have collected along the way that no longer serve us, our relationships, or our communities.

It's important to be willing to look at ourselves and say, "I know I am of great value, I know I am worth loving, but I do have the tendency to say and do certain things that don't feel good to those around me. It's time I look at these tendencies and behaviors."

What Are Your Tendencies

In order to love another, first we must be willing to trust them with things we know about ourselves but aren't yet willing or able to accept. What are these things? These things are the way we are in the world. Sometimes we think we are fully aware of the tendencies we bring into a relationship, but there are tendencies we might not be aware of at all. Have you ever told a person something about them to have them say to you, "I don't do that?" This is what tendencies are all about. We all have patterns, ways of being that we repeat over and over, time and time again. Some of us have a tendency to be very impulsive. Some of us like to talk without stopping—another tendency. We all have them. Together they create who we are. They give us our "character."

In examining your own tendencies, you might be surprised to find there are some you want to let go or change altogether. Why would you want to change a tendency? Because it might interfere with the way you really want to live your life. It may be interfering with the relationship you are trying to have. There might be things about yourself you want to change in order to survive and flourish within your present life situation. Perhaps you just want to be more open and friendly with the people around you. That's a good place to start. You might be aware of your tendency to pull away from others, but because you have decided it will be to your benefit to be more open to people you may not know, you instead work on letting go of your more reclusive tendencies. *Awareness and the willingness to change* is what it's all about—loving yourself, but letting go of the things you have created in your life that interfere with your ability to live the kind of life you want for yourself.

Begin to detach a little from how you feel about yourself and the things you tend to do in life. Don't hold on to them as if you'll have no identity left if you let them go. Be willing to look at yourself. It's easy to look at others and even judge them harshly, but this isn't about anyone else but you.

I don't always have to understand why I do what I do, but it's important I'm open to changing my way of being in the world. It doesn't mean I am of less value; it merely means my behavior is causing discomfort in another, and I want to recognize and acknowledge that. What I decide to do about it after that is up to me."

CHAPTER 7
What Kind of Relationships Have You Had?

Relationships connect us to each other. What in life can give you deeper, more meaningful rewards? This isn't relationships of the most casual types, but relationships that are based on a commitment to each other; relationships that bring people close to one another.

Ask yourself:

- What kind of relationships have I had in my life?
- What can I learn from this present relationship?
- Am I focused on learning, or am I just determined to have it my way?

Take time to evaluate your relationship. Look at what needs it meets and be aware of the needs that go unmet. What can you do about it? Anything at all? Take the time to talk with your partner about how you feel, what you think, and what you want from your relationship. What kind of a reception do you get from them? Are they willing to be open and communicate with you? Do they feel threatened? Do they pull away?

What do you want for yourself? How do you begin to have a relationship based on trust and sharing when the person you are trying to relate to won't trust you, or themselves, enough to share what they think, want, and feel? These are clues when you begin a new relationship. Decide for yourself if you really want to become involved with someone who is willing to share so little of themselves. It's helpful to make this decision early in your relationship before you become too entangled in all the strings that develop over time. What are these strings? These strings are invisible, yet very penetrating life lines that connect our bodies and our innermost self to the person with whom we are relating with on a physical and emotional basis. Once these strings develop, we will have greater difficulty pulling away from this person.

Where do your choices lie? Choices are available to you at all times, but there are certain times when it's easier to make a choice that allows you to leave someone you care about. How do you do this? By sincerely telling them what your needs are, what your concerns are about the relationship, and what you want from them but feel you aren't getting. Once you have done this, they can make up their mind whether they want to make any adjustments in their relationship with you or whether you are just going to have to settle for what you are receiving from them—or leave. At this point, you will be clearer about what you want to do.

If you are choosing to leave the relationship and feel clear about the decision, it doesn't mean it will be easy. Moments will come where you will feel pulled back toward the person you left. You might question whether you have made a mistake. Please be careful what you decide to do at this time. You could lose your courage and decide to sacrifice yourself and your well-being to be back in the relationship. What can you do once you have given up and fallen back into the relationship? You can be determined to take the best care of yourself as you possibly can.

Why does it sound like it's almost impossible to leave someone you care about but aren't satisfied with in a relationship? Because it is—it's very difficult to leave someone you care about to be alone in the world. We get so much comfort from being with another person. Yes, this person might not be what we would want them to be, but they are there and they love us. That's a lot to walk away from to possibly be alone.

Occasionally the universe works against us to pull us back with this person, or so it seems. We have set our minds on separating, but then things happen and we find ourselves wanting to be with this person. What can we do in this situation? Follow your heart. If you want to be with this person, then be with this person. However, don't expect them to change just because you have taken them back. All you can do is be present in love for them and for yourself.

Relationships are challenging *vehicles of growth*. They take you so many different directions, and at times it seems they take you to places you have no desire to be. No matter what's happening in our relationships, we always want to be able to listen within. By listening within, we will be able to keep our stability, learn what is there to learn, and move on when the time is right. We move on when the time is right because not all relationships are meant to last. Some relationships come into our lives to teach us certain things, and then when our lessons are complete, the relationship falls away. How do we know when this has happened? Because you will no longer have any energy or desire to be present with this person. The relationship dies a natural death. This doesn't mean you no longer care for or love this person, but it means it's time to let them go. You will know it in your heart. When this time does come, let the other person go as gently as you possibly can. Love them and let them go. Don't try to hold onto them. Don't try to make it work when you know deep inside it isn't meant to be. Be honest and tell them what you are thinking and feeling. Tell them you plan to leave the relationship because it's no longer full of life and love for you. Tell them what you feel.

What do you do once you have ended the relationship?

- You take the time to heal. Take the time to be alone or to be with whoever seems next. Don't force anything. Let it be; let it come into being on its own.
- Don't run out and replace this person right away to avoid being alone.
- Be patient and trust what occurs.
- Be honest with yourself about what you think, want, and feel.
- Take the time to reflect upon your life and upon the relationship you've left.
  - What is it you shared with this person?
  - What did you learn from them?
  - What do you think they gained from being with you?
  - Why was it difficult for you to let go and move on?
  - Would you do it all again the way you did it, or would you change something about your own behavior?

Reevaluating our behavior is how we learn. Anything we can learn along the way only improves our ability to be present with ourselves and with those who next come into our lives.

Be patient with yourself—and with the people with whom you have relationships. This relationship work is difficult at times. It's life, it's our life, and it's so important we participate consciously.

The work of learning from our relationships will teach us about ourselves and about the people we choose to love. Relax and enjoy yourself when you can, but when it's time to speak up for yourself, prepare yourself to do this also. It's important for you to participate in your present relationship. If you aren't in a relationship with a partner, you can practice these skills in your relationships with all the people in your life. Be willing to:

✓ Speak up and say what's on your mind.
✓ Be honest about what you think, want, and feel.
✓ Compromise at times.
✓ Actively listen and see the other person's point of view.
✓ Take time to be present in love for yourself and for the people around you.

You have a lot to do in a relationship, and a lot to share. Be ready and willing to do this work and you will see the rewards; they will be reflected in the quality of your life, your love, and your relationships.

Is It Possible to Get Someone to Love Us?

When we attempt to get someone to love us, what are we really trying to accomplish? Is it the loneliness inside we are hiding from or trying to cover up? What is it about this other person that is attracting us to them? Is this attraction mutual? If it isn't, why don't we let go and move on knowing the relationship isn't meant to be? Why do we feel compelled to continue trying to create something special with someone who may not appreciate us or truly want to put the energy into being with us that we are willing to put into being with them?

Can we really make a relationship work if the other person clearly doesn't care or isn't interested? How do we expect to have a mutually beneficial relationship when there is only one person contributing their time and energy? Our motivation requires examination.

Be willing to ask yourself:

- What do I hope to gain?
- Why am I choosing to do this to myself?
- Why do I want someone who doesn't seem to really want me?
- What is my concept of self?
- If I can truly love and support myself, why would I choose to place myself in the position of being the only contributing member of a relationship?

There is so much to learn when we choose to do this to ourselves. It can take a lot of strength and courage to walk away from someone you want even though you find their desires don't match yours. Our challenge is to let go of our dream of what we believe our relationship could be. Sometimes we are unwilling to let go of that dream because the other person seems to have a hold on us that keeps us wanting more even though they fail to give us what we need.

When we finally come to a place where we have no energy left to hold things together, we will find it easier to let go. We won't have the energy to hold the relationship together by ourselves. We might even ask ourselves why we tried to settle for how little this other person had to give in the first place. This realization is the beginning of us learning to love and care for ourselves. Having gained this awareness, we will find we no longer want to allow another person to demean or offer us less than what is necessary to have a healthier, stronger relationship. This is the start of us standing up for ourselves and being unwilling to settle for less than what we know we deserve.

Loving someone who fails to love us back is a huge lesson in learning self-love. Once we care enough about ourselves, we won't even consider settling for this type of relationship. As our love and support for ourselves blossoms, we will start to realize more and more our self-worth, and that will show in the kind of partner we attract.

Once we know what we don't want, it is easier to identify what we do want and to wait until that type of person shows up in our lives.

Past Relationships

Each relationship teaches us so much. We are sometimes fortunate to have had loving, good relationships that simply could not weather the passage of time. Whatever our history with past relationships, each one of them has taught us something. All this added wisdom enables us to move up a level or two in growth and maturity. This gives us the ability to attract healthier individuals capable of healthier relationships.

Celebrate what you have learned from past relationships, for they have helped to make you the person you are today.

CHAPTER 8
Who We Will Attract

Begin to examine the people you allow into your life. What is it about them you like? There could be some things you don't like, but you allow them to be a part of your life anyway. What are the qualities you like and admire about a person? What are the qualities you hold within yourself? It's these very qualities you will attract in someone else. This means when you can be something yourself, you will be able to attract someone else into your life who has these very same qualities. What if they are qualities you don't like? Then *the only person you can change is yourself.* Don't begin working on the other person. See within them qualities that could also be present within you. This can be difficult to admit, and at times also difficult to see.

The next time you are with someone and they do something you don't like, pay attention to what they are doing. Do you do this yourself? Are you in a relationship with someone who keeps pulling away from you, distancing themselves by not communicating their wants and needs? Do you do this? It's important we look at the behavior of those individuals we are involved with to see if what they are doing in any way reflects something within ourselves that we should change. Conceivably, you have to be on the receiving end of another's behavior to get an idea for what it feels like to be in the place of a person who experiences that behavior from you.

It's imperative we stop doing to others what we *don't* like having done to ourselves.

There can be a sense of power in what we choose to do, or we do what we do purely because we don't know better. How do we learn to know better?

1. By being placed in a situation where we experience what we do to others. The only problem is we have to be *awake and aware* of what's happening so we don't just blame the other person for their behavior and not look at our own behavior.
2. By being aware and willing to learn.
3. By being willing to talk about it with the other person. If that person is unwilling to talk, then process it within yourself or with a different friend.
4. By sharing what we are experiencing with someone outside of our relationship so we can get a clearer idea of what is really happening. When you do this, be willing to be honest.
5. Don't set the situation up to make yourself the victim. This isn't about gaining sympathy. It's about learning from the situation and from the part you play within the scheme of things.

It's important to be patient with ourselves and others. The process of being in a relationship can be difficult. It's one of great value, but also one with many challenges. When we want things a certain way and it isn't possible, we might consider leaving the relationship, but that isn't always an option either. Perhaps for some reason we have to stick it out and work through whatever difficulties are present. To do this, you need to love yourself a great deal and be willing to share your love with this other person even though you may not like what he or she is doing at the time.

How do we learn to love people without conditions? By facing the fact that we love this person no matter what they choose to do. This doesn't mean it will always be healthy to stay with them, but it does mean that in spite of it all, the love you feel for them is alive and well. We may not always want to admit we feel this love because it can be too painful. Admitting the love we hold inside continues to live and to love regardless of what occurs in the outside world is a difficult thing to do.

What should we do when the person we love loves someone else? You should do what's necessary to take good care of yourself. This will vary for each person—and for every relationship and situation in which you find yourself. We have something to learn from whatever the situation is. It could be difficult to detach enough to think about this painful experience as a learning opportunity, but it's important to do so. Once you can do this, you will realize everything that happens in your life happens to teach you something. Everything that occurs can be of benefit to you, if only you can achieve the learning potential present.

Why does learning have to be so painful? Stop and examine what is painful about the experience. *What is truly creating the pain?* Is it pain we are bringing to ourselves because we don't feel worthy of the love someone else is trying to give us? Is it pain we are bringing to ourselves because someone else doesn't feel the compulsion to be with us that we feel to be with them? Pain can be a tricky experience. Often the pain we feel is very real and can't be ignored because it's present for us to feel and to release. At times, we aren't willing to feel it and release it; instead, we continue to hold onto it, telling others of all the injuries we have incurred. Yes, everyone has challenges in their lives. Everyone at some time has chosen to love someone only to find out this person doesn't love them back. It's to our benefit to learn to live with this knowledge and get on with our lives. It's to our benefit to stop holding on to all the pain. The only way we can do this is if we start to communicate the truth of what we feel with each other.

Communication is the key that will unlock all our pain and anguish. Once this communication has been shared, we are in a better position to let go of the past and get on with our life. Don't drag the past with you; it will only weigh you down. It can also create an energy drain that won't allow you to participate in any future happiness. Do you really want that? If not, then be careful what you choose to do with your life, how you choose to live it, and where you place your focus.

Be careful to trust the people who come into your life. Trust is an important element in any relationship. When you feel you can't trust anyone, then you are alone, no matter who is in your presence. Once we can love and trust ourselves, we can pass that love and trust onto others. *It all starts from the inside and goes outward.*

Observe what occurs in your life and in your relationships. Ask yourself what you have to *learn* from this person? What does he or she have to *teach* you? It could be something small, or it could be a major life lesson. Regardless, the most important thing is that you surround yourself with the love and acceptance you know you deserve. Truly love yourself and be willing to accept yourself and your behavior. This doesn't mean you might not want to change your behavior in the future, but use it as a *tool* from which to learn.

Love yourself, detach from the experience, feel and release all the pain, and trust that regardless of what has occurred, or is occurring, you are worth being loved. Love yourself as best you can. This will only serve to improve your relationship with yourself and with whomever you become involved with at a future date.

By releasing your pain and healing your wounds, you find it easier to open your heart to yourself and to others. Having achieved a more open-hearted relationship with yourself enables you to attract others capable of the same open-hearted ability. In doing this work of inner growth, you will be able to attract healthier and more stable relationships into your life.

Love and acceptance of yourself is an important concept to grasp, for *you can't create outside of yourself what doesn't first exist within you.*

CHAPTER 9
Our Baggage

We want to share so much, but what occurs when we are unable to be the kind of person we want to be because of baggage we carry into the relationship? This baggage can really weigh us down.

How do we know if we have any baggage ourselves? We can trust that we must have picked some up along the way. What can we do about it? All you can do is be patient, loving, and kind with yourself. When you find yourself experiencing pain because of the actions of another, it's time to explore the true source of this pain. Does it come solely from the actions of the person you are involved with, or does it go way back in your life history? You might be able to get in touch with the root of this pain—or you might not. Detaching from the experience can help you understand and accept what's happening. Once you can accept and understand your life situation a little more, you will be able to move through it in a more conscious way.

It's our ability to be *conscious* of what's happening to us and the source of our feelings and reactions that will give us the tools we need to understand our behavior. Once we can gain a deeper understanding of our behavior, we will be moving closer to a time and place where we can begin to change some of the history that seems to be repeating itself. Once we make the changes within ourselves, whether it's a change in our behavior pattern or a change in the way we decide to perceive a particular situation, once this change is made, we can move on.

We create difficulties for ourselves when we fail to be conscious in our actions toward another. Perhaps they have done something that in some way harms or hurts you. What's your automatic reaction? It might be to strike back in an attempt to hurt them. What if you can watch their behavior but detach enough not to strike back. This will change the whole pattern of your behavior with them. You will then be breaking out and away from the pattern of, "You've hurt me, now I will hurt you." Once you can do this, you will be free to live your life on a more conscious, independent level from the patterns already ingrained in your relationship. It's essential to free yourself first before any kind of healing can take place. What kind of healing will take place? A healing from within your own spirit, your own presence, your own being is what will take place. You will be stopping to take care of yourself. You will no longer be inflicting your pain upon another person. Do you see how easily this can become a vicious cycle to be repeated time and time again? That's what all dramas are about: "You did this to me, so now I will do this to you."

Instead of reacting, detach, trust what's occurring, and decide how you are going to act in the situation. To stop reacting against another's behavior can be very difficult to do at times, especially if you grow angry. If you aren't aware of what's happening, and you find yourself engulfed in your anger, you might not be able to detach enough to make a conscious choice about what you are going to do next. Instead, you will react out of anger. You will bring hurt or harm to another, then the cycle will repeat on to you. What do you want? Do you want to stop it, or do you want it to continue?

How do you control yourself when someone you love does something that makes you really angry? You remove yourself from the situation. If you have to leave the scene to keep yourself from striking back, then it's time to go. If it's at all possible, it's in your best interest if you can verbally tell this person why you are leaving. Tell them you need time to compose yourself so you don't strike back in anger. If they are unwilling to let you go, then you have a challenge. You will have to decide on the spot whether you are going to wait to say the words you want to say or if you are going to let loose and possibly damage the relationship. You have a lot of choices to make along the way. Each step you take in life involves making a choice. Stop reacting to life and to each other. Take the time to think about what you want to say and do. It's time to stop hurting ourselves and each other just because things aren't going our way.

It's essential to show some restraint in our relationships and learn some control in our lives. This doesn't mean we get to control others; it means we work at controlling ourselves. It takes maturity to control what we think and choose to put out into the world. We might not always be able to do this when we find ourselves in places of tremendous anger, but we can get into the habit of finding a place to go to be alone with ourselves. When we are alone, we can't hurt someone else. Begin to look at some of your relationships. Look at how you have treated others in your life. Do you like the relationship you are in? Are you treated with the respect you think you deserve? All these things are a reflection of what you have passed on to others. If you find yourself sitting alone, perhaps it's an opportunity to learn the value of having another person present with you. Being alone does give us a chance to come to appreciate and enjoy the beauty another human being can bring into our lives.

As we work on feeling and releasing our baggage, the benefits of our healing will enable us to:

- Love each other more deeply.
- Learn to let each other go.
- Learn to love and to trust ourselves.
- Trust we can have a life we want to live.
- Start looking toward ourselves for the meaningful things in life.
- Love and support ourselves in a growth-enhancing manner.
- Be more open to learning and growing through our relationships.
- Share more of ourselves with those we love.
- Feeling and releasing our baggage makes us lighter and happier human beings. Who wouldn't want that?

Are We Afraid We Aren't Worth Loving?

What are we afraid of when we first start having a relationship with another person? Perhaps we are afraid we will like them, but they won't like us. What is it about us they won't like? We often try to figure that out ahead of time so we can hide that part of ourselves. Why do we want to hide a part of ourselves? So we will be accepted and loved. Does that sound reasonable? What does reason have to do with it; it can be something we have learned to do since childhood. If we are good, if we are quiet, if we go along with what the other person wants, then we will be loved. What kind of message did your parents leave with you? Whatever message you had with them, that's the routine you will repeat in your relationships.

Why are we so afraid we won't be loved? Do we really give all our power to another person to determine whether we are of value? We want to look at how we treat ourselves and what we are willing give up when we enter into a relationship. Are you comfortable with yourself when another person enters your life? Do you try to please them, or do you please yourself instead? There is a lot to look at when you start spending time with someone else. Perhaps you like this person, but you aren't sure whether you want to share your life with them. A lot of decisions must be made. At what point do you try to make these decisions? Some people try to make them on their first date; others wait until they've known the person for quite some time. It could be you want to have a relationship, but the person you are with doesn't meet all the requirements of someone you would like to marry. What do you do then? Do you throw them away hoping someone more suited to your tastes and your requirements will come along someday, or do you stay in the relationship and try to make it work as best you can?

You have so much to consider when you spend your time with another person. You decide each day how you are going to treat them. Do you treasure them and their company, or are you barely tolerating their presence? At times, people who would be best off letting each other go try to stay together. One of the motivating factors is fear of change; they are afraid to let each other go because their lives will no longer be predictable.

Ask yourself:

- What do we want from each other?
- What are we willing to give?
- Do I feel the other person is asking more from me than I have to share?

- What are the feelings I have about this person?
- Do I have dreams I am letting go of because of this other person's presence in my life?
- What do I really want to do about the relationship?

It can be hard to be really honest with the person you are in a relationship with because you don't want to hurt their feelings. What happens when you withhold your thoughts and feelings from them? Perhaps you are protecting them in one way but hurting them in another. It's not easy to decide what should be shared and what needs to be kept to oneself. You might stop and ask yourself what your *motivation* is for what you are choosing to do. Your motivation, you may find, is for your benefit alone and not for theirs. What does it cost you to be honest? At times, it's a great deal, and at other times, it acts as an opportunity for both people to share with each other at a much deeper level.

In order to release our baggage and also the people and things we don't want in our lives, we will find it necessary to be brave and courageous. We risk a lot when we are willing to be honest with ourselves and others. What we don't risk, however, is our relationship with ourselves. As our baggage falls away, we will find ourselves in a much better place and the people we attract will be those who have the ability to be strong and courageous within themselves as well.

There is no predetermined pattern of behavior that's effective in having a sensational relationship. All you can do is lead the way by living your life from your heart and by being true to yourself.

CHAPTER 10
Healing Past Wounds

When our wounds from the past are pressed upon, we can become quite reactive to the person pressing on them. Often we react without forethought, damaging the relationship we are in. Once we have damaged the relationship, we try to protect ourselves and then fix the damage we have done. If instead we can choose to be conscious of what is taking place and do the work of separating ourselves from the pain we feel, we can then respond from a place of healing compassion for ourselves and for those with whom we are relating.

One day at a time, we will find it of tremendous value if we can become more conscious of what we say to another, and also to the feelings we feel when someone else says something to us. This awareness will give us the ability to step back within ourselves, hear what is being said, then choose consciously how to respond. If what another says to us causes an immediate reaction within us, it's even more important that we take a moment or two before we respond. When we start to feel our emotional body reacting to the words of another, we want to ask ourselves, "Where is this reaction inside of me coming from? What is being said that is causing discomfort, if not pain for me? What can I do about it?" You can step back and 1) identify the statement that creates the pain; 2) explore within yourself why these words, why this comment, has you reacting in this way; and 3) put into words for the other person what is taking place within you at that time. When we can share with another what is happening within us, we are putting it out into the light to be healed. Putting our pain out into the light helps us discover what buttons are being pushed within us and the possible root cause of the pain. Once we can identify the cause and bring it out into the open, we can start to release it, letting it go to lighten our soul, our very presence in the world. To lighten our soul, we must unburden ourselves from the pain we hold inside. Many of us don't have a clue as to how much baggage, how much pain we carry inside. Hopefully we can identify the source of the pain, but if we can't, we might have to settle for making a statement regarding the pain, but not yet be able to dig deep enough for the source.

When we can lighten the load of pain we carry inside, we can open our hearts even further and love in a way that is deeper than we have previously been able to love. The compassion for ourselves and for others will increase. We will find ourselves more strongly connected to all the relationships we have in life. To love ourselves and to move forth in compassion will make such a difference in our journey. To heal our wounds and to be able to connect with others on a deeper level is a sacred gift beyond imagining.

Be ready to do this work of loving and letting go. We love ourselves, we love others, and we choose to move forward in our lives in a conscious way. In living this conscious life, we are better prepared to share honestly with another when their words seem to create pain within us. If we have a healthy, connected relationship, the other person will also feel comfortable sharing their pain with us. It is a great privilege to have another person trust us enough to share what hurts within them.

Heal your wounds and be prepared to live a life that lightens your soul and helps move forward all the souls traveling with you.

CHAPTER 11
Our Ability (or Inability) to Have Intimate Relationships

The relationships we build in life will serve us well for a great deal of time. What do we want from the relationships we have with those now in our life? Do you realize relationships serve a purpose? At times, the purpose of our relationship is to be a friend; other times it's not. What do we want and expect from others? What do we give ourselves? It's beneficial to understand why each person we allow into our lives is present. Once we can do this and be honest with ourselves in the process, we will begin to understand ourselves and the lives we choose to live. Why is this important? Because we gain the awareness of what is acceptable to us and what isn't. What do we allow ourselves to do with others, and where do we draw the line between friendship and acquaintance? Why do we draw this line? It's important to realize these things because in order to better understand ourselves, we want to first look at and be aware of our ability (or inability) to have intimate relationships with other people. This intimacy isn't just physical intimacy, but *personal* intimacy. How do we communicate, or not communicate, with those around us? What is the basis of our commitment to those in our lives? What do we want from others, and what are we willing to share?

At times, people come into our life, and we want to share so much with them, but for some reason, they close us out. When they do this, it can be difficult to understand why. Do we ask them why? Will they tell us? What do we choose to do with this information? Do we honor them and keep this information confidential, or do we share it with others?

Is there anything in your life that's confidential? Do you tell everyone everything you do, think, and want, or does it depend on the relationship you have with the person with whom you are speaking? *Codes of honor* exist between people who care about each other. Codes of honor protect information that is meant to be confidential. What's your code of honor? Do you have one?

Our goal is to look at our personal relationships. What do we share of ourselves? What do we choose to hide? Why are we choosing to hide something? Is it for our benefit or for the benefit of someone else? There are a lot of reasons for the things we do. It's important to start being aware of what those reasons are. If we want to have relationships where we are fully committed to revealing the truth of who we are, we want to stop hiding so much from each other.

Ask yourself:

- Why do I hide?
- What am I afraid of?
- Who am I really concerned about?
- What is the pain I think I will feel if someone else comes to know and care for me?

Occasionally, we hide from each other because it seems easier than getting to know someone and then having to let that person go. Possibly you are someone who has had a lot of people come into your life, only to leave you in a short amount of time. Are you trying to protect yourself from being abandoned again? Why do you want to do this? What are you afraid you will feel? Do you want to let go of all that's present for you to feel, and to release? If you do, first feel it; then be prepared to let it go. Ask yourself why you attract relationships that don't seem to last. Once you have done that, wait for a response. You will get an answer, perhaps in the form of a premonition, or just an instinctive response, but it will come. Acknowledge what you seem to hear or know. Listen within. The answer is there. Once you hear the answer, be willing to look within yourself so you can make whatever changes are needed. These changes will help you be more secure within yourself and therefore more secure within your relationships.

Stop Running Away

Relationships are challenges to be faced. It's important we stop running away from ourselves and from the people with whom we become involved. When we find ourselves pulling away from someone, it's of benefit to discover why we are doing this. It's time to stop saying over and over, "It just isn't the right person for me." Why isn't it the right person for you? What do you like about this person? What do you not like? What will be required of you to stay in this relationship?

We want to start analyzing our relationships more. It doesn't mean we hold onto relationships that truly don't work, but it means we gain more insight from what works and what doesn't.

Ask yourself:

- Why when I am drawn to someone, do I instead decide to pull away from them?

- What scares me about the relationship?
- What do I see happening that I would like to change?
- What is the other person doing that's bothering me?
- How good is our ability to communicate thoughts and feelings with each other?

Don't quickly pull away from a relationship unless it's one that's truly harmful to you. Decide instead to learn why things seem to go astray so easily. Why you seem to only be able to be with another person for a short time, or when they are at more of a distance from you.

Good relationship questions:

- What happens when the other person gets too close or asks too much of you?
- How do you react? Do you get scared and run away? Do you clam up and then disappear as fast as you can?
- Do you tell the other person that you have changed your mind about being in a relationship?
- Do you tell them what scared you away?
- Do you tell them what you didn't like about them or about the relationship?
- How did you handle your departure?

Many people leave relationships in a great deal of anger. Why are you angry at this other person? What did they do to offend you? Why don't you call them and try to work it out? What stands between you and them? Is it your pride, or is it a behavior they have that you know you can't accept? Why not communicate what you want, think, and feel? Why not tell them what it is about them that's difficult for you to understand or begin to tolerate? Why not use this opportunity to learn and to grow with each other?

You might not think it worth your time and energy, but it is. Call this person. Tell them what's hurtful or harmful to you. Tell them how you feel. Tell them what you think. Listen to what they have to tell you. Conceivably, they were only reacting to something you said or did. Let's figure this out. Let's try to take the time to understand why we are losing people we care about and possibly love. You may want to pull away from them and never return; that's up to you, but what do you have to lose by communicating with them one last time so you both can come to understand better why the relationship isn't working?

Things to focus on:

- Take the time to communicate.
- Try to understand the other person's viewpoint.
- Respect our own needs, but also respect the needs and concerns of the other person.
- Be willing to be kind to each other regardless of the outcome. Are we going to be nice only if it goes our way, or are we going to try to show some compassion and understanding regardless of how things turn out?
- Stop hurting each other and striking out.
- Take the time to stop and listen within to understand what our own difficulties are in a relationship.
- Let go of false pride and open up and share what we find with the other person.

This does depend on the type of relationship you have had up until this time. Is it a relationship where you can trust the other person to be kind to you during a time of challenge, or does this other person use your own words against you to bring you harm and injury?

It makes such a difference if both people involved can share their thoughts without bringing injury to each other. This requires a high level of maturity and compassion. Be concerned only about telling the truth and coming to terms with what is occurring. When you can communicate in this way, you will feel so much freedom and love. You will feel the freedom from being buried emotionally by the situation, and you will feel love for yourself and for the other person.

What Is the Relationship We Have with Ourselves?

Trust yourself, love yourself, and take the time necessary to be alone so you can get to know who you are. Why would you want to do that? So you can have a better relationship with yourself. That's the *foundation* for all the relationships you have in your life. If the foundation of the relationship you have with yourself isn't secure, then none of the relationships you build with others will be either. *It all starts with you.* It all starts with how you feel about yourself and the life you live. This doesn't mean you have to be happy with yourself or have your life in order to have a relationship, or relationships, with others, but it does mean the foundation of your relationship with others will be stronger if you know, care for, and love yourself. Those things are essential to the base of all caring, loving relationships.

Begin to observe the relationships in your life, especially how you treat the people around you. Don't expect to be treated better than the way you treat others. Learn how to take good care of yourself. Trust you have the ability to learn how to be in a relationship in a way that's nurturing to yourself and to the other person.

It's time to get to know yourself. Spend some time alone. Why are you so fearful of this? Why can't you relax and enjoy yourself without having to be entertained by someone else, or something else? Many people find it difficult to sit still for even five minutes.

Why is this? What are they afraid of? It could be they are wound up so tight from all the tension and movement in their life that they can't adjust to simply standing still for a moment or two. It's difficult to get to know yourself or anyone else when you have no time for it. When you find yourself in this situation, consider making a choice—whether to continue your present behavior or change some aspects of your life so you will have more time for yourself and for others. Our days are full of decisions and choices. It can be overwhelming at times. Instead of taking a big chunk of time off, start with taking little bits of time here and there. Learn to relax and be alone a little at a time. You don't want to overdo it and have it become an experience that's too much for you.

Take the time you need for yourself. Learn to trust, love, and care for yourself. Be willing to relax more around others. Do this for yourself; do this for the health of all your relationships. It's not possible to continue on with such a hurried life and not lose a lot of the people you care for just because you no longer have the time to love and nourish your relationships with them. Consider what has value in your life. Is it your relationships with others? Is it the work you do? *What do you care the most about?* That's the life you will create for yourself.

After you die, what do you think will live on? What would you then have wanted for yourself and for those you care about? It's something to think about because none of us are guaranteed a full lifetime to make all these decisions and choices. Choose what you feel is most important. Stand by this choice once you have made it. Trust somehow your life will work out—that you will have what you most need. But first of all, above all else, be willing to stand up for yourself and for what is important to you. Be willing to do this for yourself. Be willing to do this for your friends. Be willing to do this for the person with whom you share an intimate relationship. Care about them, but also take the time to show them you do care—they do matter to you. All this takes time. Do you have it? How will you change your life so you do? Is it possible? If it isn't, what are you choosing to place as a priority above your family, friends, or self?

It's necessary to take the time to look at our lives and our relationships—so ask yourself:

- Who can I trust?
- Who do I care about?
- Do they know I feel this way? If they don't, why don't I tell them?
- What am I afraid of?
- These important questions raise the issue of whether you are willing to be true to yourself and to the life you want.
- Do you want a life of love? One of true intimacy and companionship?
- How do you expect to have that if you keep everyone at arm's length?
- How do you expect to have an intimate relationship when you aren't able to be intimate at all? This doesn't mean you can't have a physically intimate relationship, but it could mean your ability to have a well-balanced mentally and emotionally committed relationship is compromised.
- What do you want for yourself?
- What do you want for those you love and care for?
- Do you even have the time to love and care for anyone? If you don't have this time, ask yourself why you aren't allowing this in your life.
- Why are you placing other things as being of more value, more importance?
- Do you feel your role as wage earner makes it impossible for you to sustain a lasting relationship? This could be true

if the value you place on your job is greater than the one you place on the person you care about.

Why do you have to choose? Because there will come a time when there will be a conflict of interest and you will have to choose one above the other. Be careful not to continually choose the job above the person you love. That person may not always be there. The job may not always be there either, but which one truly holds more value in your heart? Be careful what choice you make; don't just shirk it off as your duty and be unwilling to take responsibility for the choice you are choosing to make.

Looking at the relationships in our lives, we can clarify what we want for ourselves and for those we love. As we attempt to take care of our needs and try to assist others with theirs, there is so much to learn. It's imperative we stay conscious of our choices and trust that somehow we will have what we need. Our relationships are so very important. How we treat each other, and what we are willing to share, can make such a difference in the quality of our lives.

It's essential to give to ourselves as we do for others, which means:

- Taking time to be alone.
- Taking time to care about and for those in our life.
- Trusting more.
- Being willing to take risks.
- Choosing what's of most value to us. A time comes when our family and our friends must come first. Honor these occasions and trust that somehow everything else will work itself out in time.
- Loving and caring for ourselves and for each other.

It's only when we can do the work of loving, trusting, and letting go from our hearts that we will have a life we truly want to live and to share. There is a time for all things. Be conscious of what you choose for yourself and take time for those in your life. They deserve you and they deserve the love and intimacy you have to share with them.

The intimacy in your relationships will grow as you learn to love, honor, and trust yourself. Intimacy is the glue that helps to hold a relationship together.

CHAPTER 12
Being Alone

Do You Like to be Alone?
What is so threatening about being alone? Why do some people try to avoid it at all costs? What are your thoughts and feelings on this subject? Do you like to be alone? Do you enjoy the time you have to yourself when no one else is around? If you don't enjoy this alone time, what prevents you from doing so? What do you feel happens to you when you are alone? Why is it so difficult for some people and a great joy in life for others?

If we can't be alone, how do we listen within and learn from ourselves? What do we so fear that we will do just about anything to avoid being alone? Look at your fears. Be willing to confront them. Be willing to walk through them. Try to let them go over and over again. If you can do this work of letting go, you will come to realize the value and the beauty of your own soul. More and more, you will have a life for yourself that will be of your own making. You will think for yourself; you will know what is best for you. You can only have these answers if you are willing to listen within. In order to do this, it's necessary to take time to be alone.

When you first start taking this alone time, take it slowly but consistently. Don't neglect yourself. You will know inside when you need this time. Some options are to go for a walk by yourself, or you could lie in bed a little longer in the morning, or go to bed earlier in the evening. There are many creative ways to get some time for you. It's when we allow ourselves this time alone that we are really able to get clearly in touch with our innermost self. This will enable us to live our outer lives in a more peaceful manner. When we know what we feel—when we know what we want— our life takes on a whole different meaning. We are no longer struggling to get clear within ourselves about what we want and think about things. We gain peace and clarity, which helps us make it through our days.

When we don't take this time for ourselves, things pile up. All at once, we could feel overwhelmed by our life and might not know where to turn next. We may know we have to make changes, but because we aren't willing to take the time to contemplate these changes, we will live in turmoil and confusion. When we live in turmoil and confusion, it's easy for the frustration and anger to mount up in our life. The more we can release the pent-up emotions and thoughts we hold inside, the more peace we will carry inside and experience outside of ourselves.

It's a true gift to take the time to get to know yourself. Pay attention to what your thoughts are. Listen to the words that come out of your mouth. We can say things we are surprised to hear, which seem to come out of nowhere. Well, they do come from someplace. They are messages that are trying to come out from inside of us. If we aren't willing to take the time to listen when things are quiet, we will be forced to listen at some point in our lives. It's our choice to decide whether we want to learn from our life experiences now or wait until there is a crisis that will bring everything to a head.

Try to relax in a chair. Enjoy the quiet—enjoy the peace. Let your mind wander. Let your body relax. Why is this so hard? Would you rather go for a walk? Why not walk alone. Enjoy the landscape. See what new things you will notice when you are walking alone. The quiet time will allow you to think about and process things. So much value can be found in taking time out for ourselves.

What do you want for yourself? Do you want a life filled with people? Do you want a life where you are never alone? Do you want a *balance* between a life where you spend so much time alone, and a life where you are constantly bombarded by people? There is a balance, but only you can find it. You can get beyond your fears of being alone, and once you do, you will encounter some quite wondrous territory. There is a whole world of beauty that is available to you. This beauty lies within your own being. This beauty is you. Take time to find the part of yourself you so often neglect. Find the quiet, peaceful side of your nature.

What Is Loneliness?

Why do we think we need to have others in our life? Why don't we want to be alone? These are important questions. They affect the decisions we make about who we are willing to be with and who we are willing to settle for. Who do you want as a partner? Perhaps you don't feel you have much of a choice because you have never met anyone who is remotely like someone you would really want to share your life with. What do you do then? You have a choice: you settle for someone who might be tolerable, or you wait patiently to see if anyone with any greater potential shows up. What if they don't? What do you do then? What kind of a life will you have if no one shows up? Will it be a lonely life, or will you do the best you can to give yourself the kind of life you want?

What kind of a life do you live now? Do you live alone, or are you living with someone? Do you feel close to the person you live with? If you don't, how does it feel to be living with someone who doesn't fulfill your need for intimacy?

There are many ways to be alone. We can have lots of people around us and still feel alone. Being alone doesn't always have to mean no people are around—or that there's no one to share your life. Being alone has a lot to do with how you choose to perceive yourself and your life. Lots of people could be around you—maybe even people who love you a great deal—but you may still feel you are totally isolated and alone. *What you feel dictates whether you are lonely.*

What does *being lonely* mean? It means that no matter how many people surround you, you still feel alone. At times, we can be busy in our lives, distracted by so many things, and still have this lonely feeling inside. What does it take to fill this lonely feeling? It can be different for every person. One person might want someone to be by their side every minute of the day. For another person, it might mean they simply want to know they are loved and worth loving. Often, when we know ourselves to be loved, even though no one is anywhere around us, we can feel a deep and secure satisfaction within that prevents us from feeling alone. Why don't we all feel this? We don't all feel this because we all don't believe ourselves to be loved—or to be worth loving. Is it human to doubt our ability to be loved? Yes it is, but what do you want to choose for yourself? That you will be loved and are worth loving, or that you don't deserve to be loved? You make this choice, and it affects the way you treat and interact with others. People around you can sense whether you feel loved or worth loving. They pick up on this and contribute to your cause. Do you want your cause to be one of being loved—or one of doubting whether you are worth loving? Make the choice to be worth loving and stand by yourself in love and support each step of the way. Once you have done this, your life will begin to change. You will find you have a best friend, and that best friend will be you.

Feeling Isolated

What do we want from the people in our life? Do we want them to understand the things we say to them? Do we feel they do understand us? Do we feel at home and comfortable in our relationships? If we don't, what can we do about it? Perhaps there is nothing we can do. After all, how do you change another person and the way they are in the world? *The only person you can truly work on changing is yourself.* Realizing the limited nature of some of the relationships in your life doesn't mean you have to settle for these relationships. You could just be going through a period in time where the people who surround you aren't of like mind. It doesn't mean things will always be this way.

What can you do when you are surrounded by people with whom you feel you can share so little of what you feel and think? You can choose to trust the situation and do the best you can within it, or you can lose yourself in despair. What choice are you going to make? Be aware you do have a choice. What are you going to choose to do to yourself because of your life situation? Are you going to carry on making the best of a challenging situation, or are you going to give up? It might be difficult to persevere at times. It can be lonely indeed. It's quite challenging when we find ourselves alone even though there are people who surround us. There might even be a lot of love in the relationships with the people around us, but unless we are truly able to communicate with them, we might feel very much alone.

What can we do to help ourselves through this situation where we find ourselves so isolated and so alone in the world? We can remember the good times. Though it isn't good for one to live in the past, at times, it helps to remember the gifts you have received along the way. When we realize there have been opportunities for us to share ourselves with others before, it gives us hope and faith the future will bring us more opportunities. We all want to be loved. We all need those in our life with whom we want to share ourselves. What do we do when those people aren't present? What do we do when we find ourselves left alone? How do we treat ourselves? How do we choose to perceive ourselves or our lives? Do you lovingly support yourself, or do you punish yourself for not having what you want in your life?

Our work is to lovingly support ourselves regardless of our situation. We can only do this if we start to trust our lives and choose to believe there's a reason why things are the way they are, even though we can't begin to understand why. If we believe there's a purpose to the way things are, it eliminates our struggle— our resistance to our present situation. Once our resistance is gone, we can perceive the gifts in our life. There will be gifts if we look close enough. If we can focus on these gifts and make it through each day doing so, we will come out of the tunnel one day and find we have created a life of great value during a time of many challenges.

Do you want love? Do you want a beautiful intimacy? First learn to give these things to yourself. The love will be easy once you start to appreciate and value yourself. In doing this work, you will gain the things you really want in your life. They will come to you once you have laid a safe and secure foundation of love and respect for yourself. Once you have done this, you will attract people who will enjoy and appreciate what you have to share. This will happen quite rapidly when you get to a place of love within yourself. Many will want to share in your life then because the love you feel will radiate out to them.

Be patient with yourself. It takes time and energy to get to this place of self-love. It might be necessary to stop time and time again to remind yourself of your purpose. What can be of greater meaning than learning to love and forgive yourself so you in turn can love and forgive others? That's what life is all about *if you choose to focus on loving as your lesson in life.* Can you think of a greater lesson to learn? Is there a lesson of more value? Is there a lesson that has a greater lasting effect?

If you are alone, don't focus on your loneliness; instead, ask yourself, "How can I love and support myself better?" Once you can do this, your life will be full and precious no matter what occurs and no matter who is in it.

SECTION 3
SELF-CARE
SELF-LOVE

CHAPTER 13
Taking Care of Ourselves

I t's essential we learn to take care of ourselves. We do this by deciding what is best for us. Once we gain that knowledge, we will be able to live a life that will be of benefit not only to us, but to whoever is around us. Why is this important? Because we can't be a positive, contributing member of any relationship unless we can first contribute to the health and well-being of our own relationship with our *self*. To take good care of yourself and to live your life as fully as you can is up to you. You might think you can't have what you really want unless you have someone to love. What does it mean to love someone? It means to take care of their needs as well as your own. How can you do this if you aren't first able to care for yourself?

Ask yourself:

- Why do I expect to be able to do so much for someone else when I am prepared to do so little for myself?
- What do I really want and need from a relationship?

- Am I willing to grab any partner I can find so I won't have to be alone?
- Can I acknowledge that in never being alone I could be preventing myself from realizing *my greatest potential?*
- How can I reach my greatest potential if I am being held back by my relationship?
- Is it necessary for me to leave my relationship to be able to create a life for myself that's more beneficial and rewarding?
- Is it more important to love and be loved or to reach my greatest potential?
- Is it possible to have a *healthy* relationship and also reach my greatest potential?

Some people think that to love and be loved is all there is to life. There's some truth in that, but what we have to be careful about are the reasons we are choosing to love another, and at times placing their needs above ours. What do we hope to gain? What do we fear we will lose if we are out in life on our own? Do we have any desire to be out in life on our own? Why would this be important for us to experience?

If you do find yourself out on your own, you quickly realize how important it is for you to love and support yourself. When you are in a relationship with another person, you tend to depend on them for love and support. Sometimes that love and support is there; sometimes it's not. What do you do when it isn't? Then you are forced to make the decision *whether to love and support yourself.* Surprisingly enough, some people choose not to, and then when their lives disappoint them, they blame the person they are with for not giving them what they so wanted and needed.

It's essential we start looking to ourselves a little more for what we want and need. Though relationships are important in our lives, the relationship we have with our self is what's *most* important. Try to take better care of yourself. Try to be kinder and more supportive in the messages you give yourself. Stop expecting your partner to give you everything you need. Begin to give it to yourself. It's important you come to believe in yourself and the things you can do. The answers to what these things are will come to you over time. Be prepared to listen and to respond. Observe your life and the direction it goes. Don't feel you have to live your life for those around you; it doesn't work. It's not that we don't take others into consideration when we make choices, but we need to listen first to what is most in our hearts to do. Once we can do this, we will have more of a life that we want to live.

Listen within and be aware of the guidance you receive. Is there something that's important to you? Do you explore it, or do you just sit back and let it go by? Ask yourself why you are doing this. Are you taking care of yourself? What is necessary for you to do that? What are your needs? Stop letting them go for another day. Try to get what you need out of life. *Try to take the best care of yourself that you can so you in turn can care for the people around you.*

It all starts within us, not from the outside. We can't have what we want by neglecting our needs and focusing solely on the needs of another person. This doesn't work. All we end up with is a life that's empty and unfulfilling. There may be some changes you want to make in your life. Make them, and trust yourself enough to know what is best for you. Be patient with yourself, for at times, change can be challenging. Trust yourself, love yourself, and make the best life you can for yourself. Everyone in your life will benefit from this.

It's important you learn to live a life that holds meaning for you. When you can do this alone, what you will bring to a relationship will be of tremendous value. You will be free of so many needs that you would have otherwise chosen to place upon the other person in the relationship. It's not that you won't want and need the other person, but your wants and needs will be coming from a healthier, less dependent place. This will give you so much more freedom within your relationship.

Watch to see what you can do to improve your life. Do it—for yourself. Somehow it will all work out. It might seem like you are reaching for the stars, but why not? They are quite beautiful. Wouldn't it be wonderful to have a life you love to live? The only way you will have it is if you choose to move toward it and embrace the things of value to you. Now is the time to do this, so don't put it off any longer. The opportunities present for you right now might not be there in another month or two. Move forth, embrace life, and share all that's of value with the people around you. Once you can do this, you will be quite happy. Your life will no longer be one of struggle and denial. You will have what you most need—which is the love you feel. You will have that for yourself, and you will have extra to share with whoever comes into your life. Embrace your life. Share what you know to be true. Trust yourself. Care about those around you. Create for yourself the most beautiful, most caring life you can imagine. You can do this. You can do it every day.

Trust yourself enough to know there is a beautiful, wonderful life for you to live. Trust you can have this life. Trust it's important for you to experience this life. With one step at a time, you can have this life. Feel yourself moving toward and into this life. It's here for you. *Detach, trust, and let go, over and over again.* Detach from what your life is in this present moment. Imagine how you would like it to be. Don't get lost in this imagining, but realize that for you to imagine something, bits and parts of it have to be within you to experience. Each person is drawn to a whole different scenario. You are drawn to what you choose to perceive for yourself for a reason. Trust this and decide this vision is what you want. Don't close yourself off to other options that come your way, but do stay aware of what you want and what actually presents itself into your life.

Frequently, we put out requests for things we want. Later, we forget we did this, and then when what we want shows up, we are surprised because we never truly expected it. What do you want for yourself? Ask for it. Say it out loud. You can ask another person, but what's most important is that you ask yourself. Only you have the answers. Only you know what's really in your heart. What does your heart want most for you? Trust it, love it, nourish it, and watch it grow. In time, you will have what you most need. Likely not all your dreams will come true, but a great many will if you pay close attention to what you ask for and to the opportunities that present themselves.

Detach, trust, and let go. Let go of having to have everything your way. What is meant by this? It's important to be flexible. At times, we ask for something in life, then we become rigid in our expectations. Say we ask for a man in our life. In comes the man, but he isn't exactly as we imagined, so we don't want him. How rigid are you? How flexible are you willing to be? Great treasures await us, but we are unwilling to look closely enough to recognize them as such. What are you willing to give to a relationship? What are you willing to release? These are important questions. If we aren't willing to give anything and we aren't willing to release anything, it could be a challenging relationship. We want to look at our ability to give and our ability to receive. We have a lot of things to consider before we enter into a relationship with another person.

What do we want for ourselves? What do we want for the other person in our life? These are informative questions. Take time to answer them honestly and to share the answers. In sharing this information, you will be building a foundation of communication with yourself in the relationship—and also one with your possible partner. This relationship of communication will be the foundation. Build it strong. Build it with the best intentions—and while you are in the process of building it, make sure you are also taking care of yourself along the way.

To Comfort Ourselves

Do we come to ourselves for comfort? If we don't, why not? What makes it difficult to turn within for the comfort and love we need? Is it the messages we give ourselves? Is it the anger and frustration we feel? What makes it difficult for us to comfort ourselves?

Why would we look to ourselves for comfort and support when we could turn to another instead? What if the other person isn't available to you at your time of need? What do you do then? Do you turn to just anyone? Do you risk losing your relationship because you can't get what you want right when you want it? Why can't you begin to find within yourself what you would want from another?

It's possible we don't even think of turning to ourselves. What can we give ourselves that someone else can't? We can give ourselves a strong inner love and sense of well-being regardless of what occurs in our life. Yes, there are times of great challenge, but what happens when, during these times, you can *be your own best friend*? You then close the gap between needing to have your needs met by someone outside of yourself and being able to bring healing and love into your life. This is an important gap to bridge. If you bridge this gap, you will have a great deal of inner strength with which to continue on through life. This inner strength is important not only for you and for getting your needs met, but it's important in stabilizing your life. You are no longer reaching outside of yourself for what you need; you are able instead to reach within. This may sound easy in theory, but it's actually quite difficult to achieve. You have to work to get past many barriers before you can truly love and support yourself through all of life's most challenging situations.

First of all, you must learn not to give up on yourself. You are worth caring for, and you are worth loving. Give yourself this care and this love. When you can do this, you will have come a great distance. After you have made it this far, it's time to change some of the messages you give yourself. Instead of saying, "nothing will ever change," decide to say, "In time, all things change." This gives you hope and support during the most challenging of times. Things *do* change, and often for the better. To *choose* to think and believe this will help give you the inner strength to continue on in a more positive frame of mind.

How you think about yourself and the direction your life is taking is important. We tend to judge ourselves harshly for not being more successful in life. We look at the lives of people who we think have it better, and we ask ourselves why we can't have that. We can't simply because it isn't ours to have. It's important to love and to accept ourselves exactly where we are in this moment. It's this moment that reveals the truth of our own true nature. *We* aren't the things we own or the things we do. *We* are our own truth and our own beauty. *We* all are here to do different things and have different, unique experiences.

Caring for Ourselves within the Context of a Relationship

Relationships are special opportunities in our lives. We don't always appreciate the beauty and the value they hold for us. We can discover ourselves within the context of a relationship if we listen within to all the messages we receive while we are interacting with others. These messages come from within our own being. They aren't coming to us from the other person, though we may try to convince ourselves they are. Why do we want to know what messages we are giving to ourselves? We want to know because some of these messages have to be changed if they are harmful and they affect the quality of our love for our "self," and for the people around us.

When we are caught up in a relationship, the person we are involved with occasionally gets to be the one who challenges our ideas of who we think we are. Do we feel of value? They will challenge this. Do we think we are of any value in a relationship? They will challenge this too. We will be challenged to our very core. It's only by standing up to this challenge in loving support of ourselves that we will be able to truly be a part of a healthy, loving relationship.

What do you want for yourself? Do you want to hide out and not be known within the relationship, or do you want to let your guard down and be totally vulnerable to another person? What you decide will determine the quality, the depth, and the intimacy of your relationship. Each person brings varying degrees of trust to the relationship. It's only when we can fully trust ourselves that we can begin to give this honor to another person. Until we can learn to trust ourselves, we will never be able to trust that the other person truly loves us. We'll always have doubt in our mind because there will be questions within ourselves about whether we are really worth loving. Once we have solved that dilemma by loving and trusting ourselves, we can move past this place of trust to the next issue in a relationship: how much of yourself do you surrender to the relationship?

Why is it necessary to surrender anything? Because when two people come together, they have different lifestyles and backgrounds. In order for them to share time and to fit into one relationship, each person has to let go of certain things. It may be the amount of free time you have to spend with others. Time is an element that determines a lot of the changes we make in our life. Energy is another. We go where our energy and greatest interests lie. If it's in being in the relationship, then that's where we will spend most of our time. If our energy lies outside of the relationship, we will find it hard to let go of the things that matter most to us. It can end up being a tug of war. At times you will want to submerge yourself in your relationship; at other times you might want to be free of it. What causes these fluctuations in time and energy? You do, by the choices you make and how you feel.

Our ability to surrender our self and our life to another person determines how we move about in the relationship. Some people will do it with ease, but others will have a great deal of difficulty letting go of what they think is more important than the relationship itself. Some people value independence more than being in a relationship. When this is the case, it's difficult to let another person have a significant amount of your time and energy. You might do it for a little while, but then you will feel yourself growing apart and away from them—wanting to claim your own ground, your own life. It's when this happens that the challenge begins for both people.

Ask yourself:

- What do I do when I feel the person I love pull away?
- Do I let them go, or do I try to pull them back to me?
- What do I do to attempt to get them back into my life?
- How far am I willing to let them go?
- Where are my limits?
- What am I doing in the meantime?
- Do I believe in myself and trust in their love, or am I doing cartwheels in an attempt to get their attention and pull them back to me?

We all act differently in every relationship we have. The one common denominator, however, is how we feel about ourselves.

Good relationship questions:

- Do I trust I am worth loving?
- Do I feel that somehow I never seem to get it right?
- What are my thoughts when I find myself in a relationship that is dissolving before my very eyes?
- Do I blame myself?
- Do I blame the other person?
- Do I stay present in love for myself and for them and do the best I can in a difficult situation?

If we are asked to let the people we love go, how do we handle it? Do we grieve our loss? Do we get angry and bitter? How do you choose to deal with the loss of someone you once loved? Do you realize this is a decision you are making that will affect you for the rest of your life? If you choose to let the person go and send them love on their journey, you will be left with tears and some heartbreak, but you will also be surrounded by love and peace. If instead you strike out in anger trying to create as much damage as you possibly can, that too will follow you on into your life as your days continue to unfold. You will have feelings of anger, resentment, and regret. What do you want to live with? What do you want to do to yourself? We are under the misunderstanding that what we do to another, we only do to them. But what we do to another we do most deeply to ourselves.

What do you do with your anger and resentment if you don't strike out? Anger is a physical energy that requires a release, preferably by channeling it into something constructive. Some people release it through strenuous exercise, others by helping the people around them. Do feel and release the anger. If you don't, it will only bring harm to you. Cry it out, yell it out, write it out, run it out. Do whatever it takes to let it go, but don't use it as an excuse to hurt another—that will only come back to haunt you in time.

We all want love. Why is it so hard to have sometimes? Because we tend to want it only if it comes from that one special person. All sorts of love exists in this world, as do all types of relationships. It's of value to learn to identify the love that's already present in our life. So often we have a full and loving life, but we aren't aware of it because we are looking elsewhere for what we think we must have. It's to our benefit to be aware and appreciative of the friendships we have in life. No, we may not have a strong physical, intimate, loving relationship with a person we can call our partner, but we may have many loving wonderful people with whom we relate daily that we hardly acknowledge as having much value to us.

It's life changing for us to do these things:

- Pay attention to what we do have in our lives.
- Be aware of the love that exists in all our life situations.
- Stop taking each other for granted.
- Focus on the good in our lives.
- Start sharing more and more with each other.

- Make every relationship in our life one of value—one of great meaning.

When we can do this, we will have a wonderful support system for whenever life brings us challenges. We will have others by our side, people who care about us because we have taken the time to care about them.

Begin now to love and care for yourself. Make your life as special as you possibly can. You don't have to own anything to do this. This has to do with the way you act and behave in the world. Create a world of love by being it. Be love. Reach out to others. Help when you can. Support yourself when times are hard. You do this by being present for yourself in as much love as you possibly can no matter what happens to you in life.

Whether you are alone or in a relationship with another person, whether you are working, whether you are healthy or ill—no matter what, it's essential you reach out to love yourself.

CHAPTER 14
Being True to Yourself

Relationships are very complex. A great deal of love, pain, and joy is possible within a relationship between two people. What do you each want to bring to the other? You might say love and joy, but what do you bring to the other person in your relationship?

Ask yourself:

- What does it mean to bring another person love and joy?
- Does it mean I have to be a perfect person?
- Does it mean I have to do everything exactly the way the other person wants me to?
- What if I don't really know what the other person wants, and no matter what I do, it doesn't seem to be right?
- Do I then berate myself and try even harder to be the person I think I should be, or do I lovingly support myself and decide what I am going to do most of all is to be true to myself?

When you aren't being true to yourself within the context of a relationship, who are you being true to? Who do you think you are then? Are you someone anyone can trust? How can you trust a person who won't be honest with you about who they really are? Someone who fears they aren't enough unless they hide behind a mask and pretend to be other than they are? Why do people choose to abandon themselves in search of the more perfect self? Why aren't we good enough the way we are? Why do we think we aren't enough?

It's work to surrender to being who we truly are and to accept our humanness. We are all human beings. None of us are perfect, though some people may give that appearance from the outside. Don't always trust what you think and see when you meet someone and think they are so grand. They could very well be grand in some ways, but also very human in others.

Do you want to be as honest and straightforward as you can be within your relationship, or do you want to appear other than the way you really are? Your mask is going to drop at some point. What are you going to do then? Could it be you are so threatened by change that you would rather push the other person away than face your own inadequacies? Are they really inadequacies, or are they simply things you need to learn?

Do you fear you aren't good enough? That maybe the person you are in a relationship with is a better person? Have you directed all your love toward them and what is really needed is for you to begin directing more love toward yourself? No, it's not selfish to love yourself. It's necessary if you want to have a true and honest relationship with another person.

Fear of Honesty

What is the source of our fear that if we are anything less than perfect, the other person won't love us? There is a good chance this fear comes from our childhoods, from growing up trying to please our parents. Some children succeed at it while others fail.

What did you have to do to please your parents? Did you have to be quiet and learn to keep your thoughts and your feelings to yourself? If you did this, then how do you change your ways now? It's possible if you are willing to work hard. Perhaps you failed to earn the love of your parents because you were always doing or saying something they didn't like. What do you do now when you are in a relationship with someone you don't want to leave you? Do you sacrifice yourself, or do you let the other person really come to know you, knowing you may indeed lose their love and acceptance? It takes a lot of strength and courage to put our concerns aside and to be as completely ourselves as is humanly possible.

Doing this work for yourself requires a certain level of inner love and support. At times you might want to give it all up and run away to be safe by yourself. What does it mean to be safe by yourself? It's one's ability to be alone and feel totally accepted. We can convince ourselves that we have little inner work to do when we aren't in a relationship and coming up against another person's words, thoughts, or feelings. When we are alone, it can feel comforting and safe. When we are with someone who doesn't like or approve of our behavior, we can feel threatened or insecure.

What do we do with these feelings of insecurity when they arise? We can feel them— then let them go. Just because they're with us doesn't mean we have to lose ourselves in these feelings. Feel them and let them go. Give yourself loving and supportive messages. Even though you may be feeling insecure and unloved in this moment, the reality you want to experience is one of being of great value and worth great love. Tell yourself this. Know deep inside that you deserve this love. Surround yourself with all the love you possibly can. In a sense, we are doing the work to reparent ourselves. We want to teach ourselves that no matter what, we deserve to be loved. Until you are willing to truly love and honor yourself, you won't be able to give what you don't have within yourself to another person.

Honesty…in Your Relationship

The relationship you have with yourself makes all the difference in the types of relationships you can have and cultivate with others. If you aren't able to be intimate and honest with yourself, you won't be able to be these things with another person.

We want to start looking within for answers to some of the questions that puzzle us in our relationships. We can do this only when we are first willing to be honest and responsible with and to ourselves. Unless we are honest with ourselves, none of the introspection we attempt will make a difference.

What do you want? Do you want truthful, honest answers, or do you want to always feel comfortable—to feel that no matter what you do it's always the right thing? Really look at what you want and the amount of discomfort you are willing to experience in order to have it. Some people are unwilling to let down their masks to let anyone, themselves included, know what they are really up to or about.

It's time to let go of what you think you should be in order to be accepted by those around you. Instead, be willing to love and to trust yourself regardless of your situation and your past behavior. Past behavior is gone; let it be in the past. Build your life forward from this present moment.

You may not always be clear in the direction your life needs to take, but if you are honest with yourself and willing to look at the consequences of your actions, you will be taking a path that will bring you deep rewards.

CHAPTER 15

What We Deserve

D o we deserve to be happy? Do we deserve the pain that comes our way? What do we think we deserve? Once you can identify what you think you deserve, you will be able to move forth from a more informed base. Take what you think you deserve and change it to what you want for yourself. That's what you truly deserve. It doesn't mean you will get it, but it does mean you value yourself and your life.

What we think of ourselves and of our lives matters. Do you think you are worthy of the love you want in your life? If you aren't worthy of the love, why not? Tell yourself all the reasons you don't think you deserve to be loved by another person. Once you have done this, look at this list to discover what would be helpful to learn to love and accept about yourself. Once you can learn to love and accept yourself, these obstacles will be removed from your path. You are a human being. You aren't perfect. You may have made mistakes along the way. What are you going to choose to do about those mistakes now? Are you going to carry them with you through your days, or are you going to find some forgiveness in your heart? Once you can forgive yourself, you will forgive others in your life too. You will have opened your heart to yourself, which is necessary if you want to find any love or light in your life.

Once we can love and forgive ourselves, we can move on to what's next to experience. Once we can release the pain we hold inside because of something we once did, we can move on into life instead of holding fast to the pain we feel because of something we can no longer influence or change. This is part of learning and growing from what we experience. In order to learn and to grow, we have to make adjustments within ourselves so we don't repeat old patterns and recreate for ourselves what we are trying so hard to forgive.

Ask yourself:

- What do I need to forgive myself for?
- Have I brought great pain to others?
- What do I find difficult to love and accept about myself?
- Do I consider myself a failure in life? Look at the expectations you hold.
- Why do I think I should have all the answers? Is it because I want to protect myself from making any mistakes along the way?
- What do I call a mistake?
- What do I want from myself? Perfection isn't necessary in order to be loved.
- Why do I find it so hard to accept myself when I do something I later regret?

We do have free will. Free will means we can change our behavior at any time and in any way. It doesn't mean we will always be successful in making the changes we want to make, but it does mean we have the ability to try. What more can we ask of ourselves at this time? If there is something about yourself you want to change, change it and move on with your life. Stop living in the past and holding on to your mistakes as if they are the only thing of value. Let go, move on, and create for yourself a life of love and light. Each moment of each day is an opportunity to start fresh again. Wake up in love for yourself. Go to bed at night in love for yourself. Be kind to yourself. Forgive yourself. Move on with your life.

Why do we try to hold on to past pains and injustices? Is it because this is how we have come to define ourselves? Is it because it gives us something to talk about and with which to relate to others? Why do you hold on to your pain? Yes, you may be divorced, but does that mean you have to relive that experience for years afterward? Yes, your husband or your wife may have left you for another person. If they did, accept it and move on with your life. Feel the pain and anger that comes with such situations, but be willing to let go of the past and move forward. It does take time, but it also takes commitment. It takes your commitment to letting go of the past. It takes your willingness to release yourself from being the victim in the situation. Victims get a lot of sympathy along the way. That could be hard to let go of; after all, if you let go of that, what will be left? Possibly what's left is an emptiness you will have to face. Have the courage to do this letting go. The sooner we can heal ourselves, the faster we will be able to move back into life. Healing the parts of ourselves that are broken brings us greater inner strength. We will then begin to be in a place of giving instead of a continual state of need. There will be a change in the flow of energy. Instead of us taking it in from others, we will be able to be a life force that contributes not only to our own well-being but also to the well-being of others.

If we are willing to open ourselves to feeling and releasing our pain, we can heal ourselves. Participating in this healing process can be challenging, but why hold on to the pain and bury it inside of you? You might think that if it's out of sight, it's out of mind. Eventually, something or someone will come along and they will touch upon this pain. When they do, you will react in a strong, potentially negative way. They have found your sacred spot. The place you hold your pain, where your fears lie and where you need to heal; the place you try your best to keep out of sight. Our work is to face our fears and heal our pain. When this pain arises, feel it and let it go. If we can verbally say to ourselves, "I feel this pain and I choose to let it go," we will be surprised at the effect it has upon our lives. It will heal us in a place where once we were broken. We will be able to love and accept ourselves in places we weren't previously able to venture. We will be able to be with others in a more compassionate, intimate way. We will be less afraid of protecting ourselves. It will change the way we are in the world. It will make us a more loving, compassionate, kind person because we will be able to first of all be these things to ourselves. Once we can do this for ourselves, we can do it for those around us. This will change all the patterns and relationships in our life. We deserve this healing and the love it brings to us.

By living consciously, we have a chance to heal our inner demons and to move forth into the light further and further. We will move into the light and the love we know exists within our hearts. We will move forth into the compassion of the world. But until we can see and recognize these things within ourselves, we won't be able to find them outside of us.

We Deserve the Life We Are Willing to Create

Trust your ability to love and to be loved. You may not always feel you deserve the good things people do for you. Why is this true? Why don't you feel you deserve every good thing that comes your way? Maybe you think you deserve only hardships because that's a lot of what your life has been about up until now. Sometimes what we want for ourselves is much different from what we think we deserve. Were you told as a child that you don't deserve good things because you didn't behave in the manner expected of you? What do you think about your behavior as a child, and about your life now as an adult? Is there anything different about your life presently, or are you still trying to be the "good" person so you can win everyone's approval? Yes, we all want to be loved and approved of, but what are we willing to do to ourselves in order to get it? Do we sell ourselves out? Do we end up doing things in life we really don't want to do just to be "good" people? What are you willing to do to win the approval of others? When do you stop and stand up for yourself?

We are asking a lot from ourselves when we want to choose a road no one else wants to travel.

Ask yourself:

- Am I willing to go that road on my own because I know deep inside of myself that's the only way I will have the kind of life I want to live?
- Am I willing to stand up for myself?
- Am I willing to be different from the person next to me?
- What am I willing to do to lovingly support myself in the things I know are important to me?

Life asks a great deal from us when we are placed in a position of having to decide whether to win the approval of those we love by doing something we don't want to do, or by remaining true to ourselves and realizing no one will understand. It's hard when those we love seem to turn against us because we are making choices they don't agree with. What do you do? Do you surrender to their demands, or do you continue on your way?

If we can believe our lives are exactly the way they need to be, and we are to learn from our current life situation, it's of value for us to:

- Stop wanting to be somewhere else and start being exactly where we are.
- Move forward only from this present moment. It's only *now* that we can experience.
- Make our life as good as it possibly can be.
- Think positive thoughts.
- Take time for those we love and care about.
- Take time to be alone with ourselves.
- Love and nurture ourselves as well as the people in our life.

When we can do all of these things, we will have a full and rewarding life regardless of our life situation. We deserve to create a good life for ourselves.

Don't let your life situation define your experience. The two are not necessarily connected.

CHAPTER 16
Our Life Dreams

What are your life dreams? If we grow too far away from our life dreams, we will lose our enthusiasm for the life we live. What can we do to help ourselves recapture our love for life? Pay attention, listen within, trust yourself, and be willing to ask for what you want. In order to ask, you need to be aware of what you want. Do you know what this is? Is a life full of meaning what you want? What means something to you? What would this expression be for you? Realize it will be different for each person you know. Trust yourself and be willing to move toward your dreams. You can have them if only you are willing to give them to yourself. You can only do that by being true to your own inner being. Listen within; trust you can have what you most want in life, and be prepared to ask for it time and time again.

Why must we ask for something time and time again? Because it takes time for things to come through to you. Maybe you don't realize the density of matter and how difficult it is to create from your thoughts alone. Much more must accompany your thoughts.

It's imperative you 1) have the intention of someone who wishes to succeed, 2) be willing to risk what you have, and 3) be willing to let go of what is present in your life so what needs to come into your life can do so. One step at a time you can do this. Trust your needs will be met. Trust you are beautifully cared for. Trust what you want is possible. Move forward in trust of all that occurs and your life will be revealed to you a little at a time. It may be a life you recognize to be yours because it's something you have wanted for so long, or it may be very different from what you expected. Regardless of what is present for you, it's important you learn to accept yourself and your life.

What are you going to do if your life turns out much different than you anticipated? Are you going to try to make the best of it, or are you going to throw it all away? It's totally up to you. Realize, however, you are not alone in your experience. Many, many people are connected to you. All of those people will be affected by the way you embrace or reject your life and yourself. You will be teaching them how to be in this world through your behavior. Suddenly it changes from "How am I going to handle this situation?" to "How can I deal with this so all the people I love can also accept this situation?" You are no longer a single unit acting alone; you are a group of individual people who are *deeply connected* to each other.

Our dreams are important, but they aren't the only thing that is. It's the people in our lives that love and support us that hold the greatest value of all. When we can figure out what our dreams are, yet continue to include others in our lives in a way that is beneficial to all, it makes our dreams even more rewarding if or when they do come true.

To have our dreams come true at the cost of our relationships might make what we have to gain of less value to us. Our focus can include both our relationships and what we are trying to achieve for ourselves. Balance is what we want to maintain. Balance of thinking about ourselves and the direction we want our life to take, and balance in the time and energy we put into our relations with others.

When our dreams fail to materialize, we can find ourselves quite discouraged. We can talk to those in our lives and share our thoughts and feelings. When our dreams change, we can identify the steps we can take to move us in that particular direction. Sometimes we fail to follow through on our part of making our dreams come true. Could that be because we fail to believe in ourselves and our ability to create an amazing life for ourselves? When this occurs, if we can recognize the places within ourselves we want to shore up and strengthen, we can make more progress on what we next choose to do.

Dreams are interesting things. For some people's dreams change on a daily basis, yet for some they have a sense of what their purpose is and can create the outcome they want to experience. When our dreams take over our lives and we fail to be with the people around us that we value, we risk the chance to maintain strong and healthy relationships. Balance your drive and ambition with your love for those you value. We want to combine both our love for life and our love for those in our lives.

Dreams come and go but the people who are most important remain true to us if we remain true to them.

SECTION 4
OUR NEEDS AND EXPECTATIONS

CHAPTER 17
Identifying Our Needs and Expectations

I t's time to look carefully at the relationships we have in our lives. What do you appreciate about the people with whom you spend time? What do you give to each other? These exchanges are the basis of all relationships. You must have something to give the other person and them you—or there would be no reason to come together. Look at what you want and need from another person. Look at what you appreciate about them. These are the qualities that mean the most to you. Are they qualities that symbolize what you most want in life? Be careful here because we can be drawn to people for the wrong reasons—not so much because we love and care for them but instead because they have something we want from them. What do you want? Is it something that will truly improve your life?

Look at what you want from another person. Can you bring these things into your life on your own? Doing so would bring you freedom because these are the reasons you *need* another person in your life. Wouldn't it be wonderful to be free from *needing* another person in your life? This doesn't mean you won't want a relationship to have someone to share your life with, but *needing* and *wanting* are two different things.

What do you need from another? What do you want from another? When your actions are driven from a place of need, it's not always easy to be true to yourself. You might choose to surrender your own identity because it will get you what you think you need. When you want something, it leaves you the freedom to choose what you are willing to do to get it. *Wanting* doesn't put you in a place of surrendering your own needs as much as *needing* does. Wanting is a desire, but not as compulsive as needing. When you need another person in your life, it's as if you can't live a full life without someone else there. This handicaps you and your ability to live your life from a place of honor within you. When you simply want someone in your life, you can choose to let go of that want and get on with your life—the ability to do so is very important. It doesn't do anyone any good to sit and pine away because you don't have that one special person in your life.

What do you want for yourself? It's important to realize that wanting something doesn't mean you will always get it. There's a great freedom in wanting something, or someone, and then being able to actually release them and let them go. When you do this, you have to stand on your own two feet. When one stands on their own two feet, they are choosing to have the strength and love to care for themselves regardless of whether someone else is in their life. Unless we can love and care for ourselves, how do we expect to truly benefit from any relationship?

When you can be your own best friend, you will be able to care for yourself within the context of all your relationships. Relationships are valuable ways to learn more about ourselves and those with whom we share our lives. Each of us has a unique and interesting personality. We all are here with different missions. Some of us to learn more about loving ourselves, others to be of service, etc. There are many, many reasons for being here, as many as there are people on this planet.

Our ultimate aim is to learn to love each other. How can we do this for each other if we can't do it for ourselves? Perhaps it's just the physical relationship you miss in your life. What do you hope to gain by having a physical relationship with another person? Yes, it may feel wonderful for a short period of time, but then the reality of their personality *wants and needs* begin to surface. Demands are placed upon us we might not be willing or able to meet. The work here is to be honest with ourselves as to what potential this particular relationship holds. Often there is little to no potential, but we work hard to keep the relationship going. Sometimes great potential exists, but we throw the relationship away because we are afraid we don't deserve it.

We are all complex human beings. The more we can love and trust ourselves, the deeper and more wonderful our relationships will be. Once we can truly love ourselves, we will be able to stand back and deal with our relationships in a more detached manner. This ability to detach more will enable us to work on issues that arise. Working on these issues contributes to the strength and endurance of the relationship. The relationship can only be as strong as you are. It can only survive the lessons in life you are able to absorb and process. If you live in fear, you won't be able to work out much of what comes to you. If, however, you have a good basis of self-love and trust for what's occurring, then you will be able to detach and understand the lesson that's present for you to learn.

Loving is about learning. We can't love another without learning a great deal about them. They love us back, but we can only truly feel it in as much as we are able to love them. The depth of our emotions depends on our ability to be true to ourselves and to commit ourselves fully to the relationship. You can't expect to have a full and wonderful relationship if you always have one foot on the ground, ready to run or escape. You might instead ask yourself why you would want to run or escape. What is causing you to run—and what are you escaping to? Some of us think if only we can be alone, then we will be safe. You might be safe for a while, but life has a way of bringing us our lessons no matter what our situation is as far as relationships go. We will learn whether we are in a relationship with someone or if we are on our own. The lessons we learn will just be different.

We can think the other person wants too much from us. How can we tell if their wants and desires are realistic? Does it matter whether they are realistic? What does matter is what's going on within us. What are we thinking, what are we feeling? It's of value to be honest with ourselves and with the other person. It's in this honesty we will discover the *pain* that could be hidden under our present behavior. We will be forced to face our pain and our fears. When we can face our pain and fears in a relationship supported not only by ourselves but by the other person as well, it's a beautiful, intimate experience. It's an extremely healing experience too.

It's time we come together and heal ourselves of all the wounds we have suffered. It's only by allowing ourselves to be vulnerable to another that we will be able to do this. This other person may not always be there for us, but what we have to make sure of is that we are always there for ourselves. We do this by being compassionate and kind to ourselves regardless of the situation. These lessons can be tough, and the challenges we meet might bring us to our knees, but what matters most is how we treat ourselves. Our partner will pick up clues from us. If we are ready to abuse ourselves, they may stand in line to contribute more to the cause. If we support ourselves in kindness and love, our partner could choose to do the same. We can't always depend on the person in our life to take care of us…we need to learn to do that for ourselves. Once we can do that for ourselves, the added concern and support our partner gives us will be that much more appreciated and treasured.

We want also to be aware of the person in the relationship with us and what their needs are. It can be so easy to get caught up in our needs that we don't pay attention to what their needs are. They could have needs that require attention at the same time we have needs that aren't being met. Who gets their needs met and in what order? Are you constantly putting your needs aside for them and their needs, or is there a balance to what occurs in your relationship?

At times, we expect so much from the other person. We expect them to be there close to us at every turn in the road. This isn't always possible, and it would be helpful to the relationship if we can cut them some slack—and realize they could have things going on in their life that are greatly challenging them. When this occurs, you might have to put your needs aside and let them know you support them in what they are trying to do. You will realize you are trying to support them at your own expense if you feel resentful. If these feelings arise, be honest with yourself, and if possible share your thoughts with this other person. You then may choose to change your behavior within the relationship to balance out your needs.

Relationships are challenging; some are of incredible growth value, and others aren't. What's happening right now within your relationship? Do you want to stay in the relationship? Do you want to leave it? If you are waiting for a relationship, what are the needs you hope it will fulfill? Take this time to decide for yourself how you can best live your own life. This will be helpful, whether you find yourself in a relationship or not.

Love yourself more fully. When you can do this, you will find that love spilling over into all of your relationships. There is a lot of work to be done to clear ourselves of the unnecessary expectations we carry. Awareness of what these expectations are is the beginning; from there, we gain control of how we choose to participate in this new, healthier version of our relationship.

Working through Our Expectations.

What do we expect from each other? Do we expect proof that we are worth loving? What happens when this proof isn't there? Do we automatically assume we aren't of any importance, that we really don't matter? Often this is exactly what we do. Because another person doesn't find us appealing, we think our value is in question. Why do we do this to ourselves? Why do we think that if another person doesn't care for us, we shouldn't care for ourselves either? We have it all turned around.

Ask yourself, "What do I want from another person?"

- Is it approval for who I am and what I do?
- What do I expect the other person to give me that I am unable to do for myself?
- Do I expect them to give me the love I want but so far have been unable to find?
- Where have I looked for this love? Have I looked within myself, or have I only looked to another for it?

- Do I listen within and acknowledge the needs I feel are unmet?
- Do I want to live my life struggling to get what I want and need from another, or do I want to ask myself how I can better meet the needs I have?

There will be times when what you want and need from another is truly legitimate and of concern, but often we place our needs upon another when we are the only person who can really meet them.

It's important for us to be aware not only of what our needs are, but also the needs of another. Perhaps we don't think their needs are as important as ours, but they are. They are very important. This person we live with, or spend our time with, is of great value. We are of great value. Do you love and honor this person each and every day? Do you love and honor yourself each and every day? If you do, that's wonderful. If you don't you might ask yourself why.

In your present relationship:
- What do you find missing?
- Whose fault is it that it isn't there?
- Could it be you haven't tried hard enough?
- Could it be deep down you don't really care that much?
- What is holding you back from having a fully committed, loving relationship?
- What are the differences in your life that bring you together?
- What are the differences that seem to tear you apart? Look at these differences. What do they mean? What do they have to teach?

It could be you thought you'd meet someone and live happily ever after—but that isn't what has happened. Why were you so disappointed to find out this person you love is an ordinary human like yourself? You wanted them to be bigger than life, possibly you thought they were, only to find out later that they have flaws just like you do. What kind of person did you expect to attract to yourself? Someone more perfect than you are? Is that possible? If it isn't, what do we have to learn from this situation? Perhaps what we should learn to do is to love ourselves and love this other person regardless of the flaws and differences that are there. We are flawed. Why should the person we are involved with be any different? It's essential we all learn to trust and love ourselves so we can trust and love those around us.

What does it mean to trust and love ourselves? It means we realize our value no matter what's happening in our life. We realize we are worth loving—we don't doubt that. When we can trust and love ourselves, our lives will operate a whole lot smoother. All the times that challenge you will find you standing there strong within yourself. This doesn't mean you are called upon to be stubborn—there's a difference. To be strong means to be open to what's occurring but to trust you will be fine no matter what happens. To be stubborn means you are determined to set yourself against whatever occurs. Our goal is to be flexible, yet also to be strong within our own being.

Ask yourself, "What are the situations that arise in my life that challenge me, and how do I handle them?"

- Do I depend completely on the person I am involved with to take care of everything for me?
- Do I go to the other extreme and not allow this person to have any say?
- How do I react when something occurs that challenges me to my very core?

- Am I able to discuss the challenge honestly with my partner, and if not, why not?
- What do I do when I want help and support?
- As a couple, are we able to depend upon each other? If you are, how does this feel?
- How does it feel to be closed out when experiencing a time of need?

All of this is part of a relationship. As much as we always want to be there for the person we love and share our life with, it isn't always possible. We don't live in a vacuum. While things are happening in our partner's life, things are also happening in our life. At times in all relationships, you find yourself a bit stranded and having to handle your life on your own. What do you do when this occurs? Do you get angry at the other person for not being there for you when you needed them, or do you ask them why they weren't able to be there? It's to our benefit to stop reacting off of each other and begin to communicate. It's important to ask for information before we attack the other person for what we needed and seemed not to get from them. A lot is going on in all our lives. It's to our benefit to 1) be more patient and understanding, 2) communicate clearly with each other, 3) trust we are worth loving no matter what occurs, and 4) detach, trust, and let go, over and over again.

What is meant by *"detach, trust, and let go?"* It means you *detach* from the experience, from the situation at hand. Once you do this, you can look at things from a more neutral place of being. You are no longer attached to a certain outcome and your emotions are no longer controlling your behavior. The next step is to *trust* what's occurring and view it as an opportunity to learn and grow. Once you can do this you will be less attached to getting the outcome you determine to be the *right one.* You will be more open to being guided through the experience. Once you have established your ability to detach and to trust what's occurring, you must be willing to let go. By *letting go,* this doesn't mean you walk away from the situation; it means you participate, but from a position of being the one who has something to learn. You let go of your grip on everything; you let go of your desire to control what is happening. This will make a big difference in your experience and also the outcome of the event. Be willing to do this for yourself; be willing to do this for the person you love.

To be present in love for another and to trust everything that occurs is quite a challenge. It will change the way you perceive your interactions with others. Try this, one day at a time, one step at a time.

Blaming Another for Us Not Having the Life We Want

Relationships are tricky things. We could decide to blame the person we are with instead of taking responsibility for our own life. If you desire something, why do you choose to ask the person you are sharing your life with for it, instead of providing it for yourself? Begin looking at this issue of blame. Do we blame another for what we should give to ourselves? We can't expect another person to make our life a happy one. It's our responsibility to do that and to make the most of each day we live.

What can we do to make our life better? What can we do to bring to ourselves the things we want? The first step is to identify what we think is missing. Be clear and be specific. What can you take responsibility for to see that you move closer to having what seems so important to you? Perhaps it's communicating with your partner what you are thinking and wanting from your relationship with them. Maybe it's something material that you should take the responsibility for achieving. Whatever it is, don't blame someone else but take responsibility for what you are willing to create or not willing to create in your own life.

When we take responsibility for our choices, for the life we live, we free our partner from expectations that would otherwise burden the relationship. We also move closer to having a more balanced exchange between both parties.

CHAPTER 18
Matching Wants and Needs in a Relationship

Relationships are ways to become better acquainted with yourself. If you trust what occurs in your life on a daily basis, you will begin to trust the people who are attracted to you more. You will begin to understand you have something to share with them, and there's also something for you to learn. When we can be more open to our learning experiences, relationships take on a whole new perspective. It's no longer a question of "What can I gain by being in this relationship?" Instead it's "What I can learn from being in this relationship?" It's important we ask ourselves this question, then stand back and watch our own behavior when we interact with another person. It's important we learn to be more effective in our ability to communicate, understand, and share with other people. These issues are pivotal if we want to understand who we are and what we have to share with anyone who comes into our lives.

What do we want for ourselves? Do we want a relationship that's quiet and content? Do we want a relationship that keeps us on our toes? Would you be surprised to know that each person wants something different depending on their needs, priorities, and values? So what you want in a relationship may not be what the person you are in a relationship with wants from you. This isn't something we usually stop to think about, or even to question. If you want a quiet relationship with someone who is prepared to be your best friend, you want to ask the person you are involved with if this is something they want too. If it isn't, you may have a choice to make. They might want something more passionate and exciting than the relationship with you presents. We all have different levels of comfort depending upon the level of stimulation we require. Matching comfort levels in a relationship creates balance and harmony.

If you match someone who requires very little stimulation with someone who requires a great deal, you will have two people who are continually trying to manipulate the other into living the lifestyle they feel is necessary to their own health and well-being. This high degree of imbalance in the relationship will require major compromises on both people's parts. The couple's ability to share with each other will influence the degree to which they are willing to compromise.

What do we want from our partner? Whether we recognize it or not—we want a lot. We want them to be the way we would like them to be so we can live with them in a more relaxed manner. When they fail to compromise with us, or when they fail to see things our way, we can become frustrated with them and with our own lives. Our challenge is to become accustomed to living with this other person who may or may not have our best interests at heart. It's possible for two people who live together and who love each other to be so totally mismatched that it will cause nothing but continual strife between them. Personalities play a big part in whether we can truly live with each other in a peaceful, loving climate. So many variables must be taken into consideration when you choose to live with someone. Just because you love this other person doesn't mean your needs will automatically be met, nor will theirs.

What do we do when we find our needs aren't being met? We become disillusioned. We have to be able to refocus on our relationship so we can discover where our difficulties lie. What is it about this other person that's making it impossible for us to continue living with them in a peaceful way? What is causing the upheaval in our lives? What would we like to change about ourselves—or about this other person? Once we can identify the problem areas, we can discuss them with our partner. If they don't agree with us, then we are left to deal with the situation on our own. Our choices might be fairly harsh. We might decide to postpone making a big decision until we know more about this person. What if we find out we really can't live with this person, but it's too late because we are already married to them? Then a decision is required. What means the most to you? Do you want to continue on in a marriage that will only grow more unsettled as time goes on? Or do you want to take time out for yourself to come to terms with what is occurring in your life? You don't have to automatically leave this person, but you can take time out. You can take time to go somewhere to be alone to contemplate what your next course of action should be. At times, this is enough to bring some enlightenment to at least one person in the relationship. If some sort of pact can be agreed to, maybe there is a way to save your marriage.

Imbalance in a Relationship

Relationships require a great deal of time and attention. You can only neglect the person in your life for so long before they begin to grow away from you. If you have a relationship you treasure, do you want to lose it? If you say you don't, what do you do to keep it healthy? How much time are you willing to spend with this other person? Is it enough? Do they seem to always want more than you are willing to give? What seems to be the balance or imbalance of your relationship?

It's possible you don't feel the necessity to be with your partner as much as they feel the desire to be with you. What do you do to compromise when you find yourself in this situation? Are you willing to compromise, or do you tell them they have to find a way to live with it? How much do you really care about this other person? Maybe you like having them there, but you really aren't concerned about what they want. You've convinced yourself that somehow they will adjust to the way things are, or if they can't, you will be better off without them. What do they ask from you? What are you willing to give?

Sometimes we are willing to give so little of ourselves to the other person. We expect them to go along with the pattern of our life. What about their life? What about their wants and desires? How can the other person be of any value to you if you aren't prepared to consider them? What do you tell yourself when you continually deny their wants? Do you think what they want isn't as important as what you want? Do you always think you know what is best for the both of you? How much of a voice are you willing to give them? Do you deny their existence until you want something from them, or do you worship the ground they walk on? Perhaps you tread somewhere in the middle.

Both people must be considered. Not only one voice should be heard; there are two people—two voices. These voices won't always agree, so be willing to compromise. You can't always dig your heels in and have your way unless you are totally unconcerned about the harm you bring to the other person.

It's time to be more conscious in our relationships. It's time to be more honest, not only with the other person, but also with ourselves.

Ways to improve our interactions with others:

- Hold back from manipulating the situation and the other person. At times we will get our way; other times we won't.
- Learn to relax more with all that occurs.
- Stop taking our emotions out on each other.
- Take time to be alone.
- Consider what we want before we share it.
- Be conscious and aware of the words we choose to use and how we say them.
- Be willing to compromise more in our relationships.

It's only when we can do these things that there will be more peace and harmony in our world.

Detach a little from the other person in the relationship. This doesn't mean you should love them less, but it does mean you should love yourself more. Take a vow to love and cherish yourself. This doesn't mean there won't be changes to make in your behavior at a future date, but it means you love and accept yourself the way you are right now. That is important. It gives your relationship with the other person a more solid base to move forth from.

What do we want and expect from each other? What are we willing to be and to do for ourselves? Perhaps we are unwilling to do anything for ourselves and expect the other person in our life to provide all the love and stimulation. What do you think will happen to a relationship that depends solely upon one individual instead of both people? *You can't have a relationship that feeds only one person.* It won't be long before the other person resents you for your continual needs. Our work is to separate enough to allow our own inner selves to shine—and to make friends with ourselves. We have to trust, love, and honor ourselves. When we can do this, we are in a position where we actually have something to give and to share with someone else in our life.

When we can have a relationship built on trust, love, and respect, usually that means *two* people are willing to lovingly work at the relationship they share. These people will put forth the effort and energy to communicate with each other and to see that not only their needs are considered, but also the needs of the other person. This consideration is essential to any good relationship. Without these elements, you will be strongly pressed to continue on in your relationship for any length of time.

We are all beings of light. We are quite beautiful in many, many ways. We have so much to give to ourselves and to share with others. A balanced give and take in a relationship allows the beauty of life to shine through.

CHAPTER 19
What Do
We Settle For?

What do you want from a relationship? Do you want to have fun and light times with another person? Do you want someone to hold you when times get rough? What do you want from this other person? What are you willing to settle for? We can be drawn to someone who gives us anything and everything except what we want for ourselves. What do we do when this occurs? Do we trust we are worth loving and move on to something or someone else, or do we hang on to the person we are with simply because we have needs—and they seem to fulfill at least a few of them?

What do you want for yourself? What are you willing to settle for? Do you see other couples around you that are happy with their relationship and with each other? Possibly you've not had these role models. What do you do when you know what you want for yourself is much different from what you are getting? Do you trust there is someone out there for you, or do you think you have to settle for the situation at hand?

It's hard to believe you can always have what you want in a person. We might think we have to settle for what comes our way.

Ask yourself:

- What if it seems no one comes my way?
- Do I trust myself and what I want in life, or do I try to get someone else to get it for me?
- What am I willing to do to not be alone?
- What am I willing to sacrifice to have another person in my life?
- Are there so few relationships in my life that I've decided to settle for this one?
- Is that the way I want someone to choose for me to be in their life?

Do you want someone you can love? Someone who will love you in return? *Loving* is a basic element to all meaningful relationships. Does the person you are with love you in the way you want to be loved? Please be honest with yourself. Do you love your partner in a way they want to be loved? Do you seem to satisfy each other's every whim? If not, why not? Perhaps that's not the reason the two of you came together. Why do couples come together? What do they have to gain from each other's presence? Often, it's companionship, but when that isn't possible, it could be just to have someone else there in your life.

At times we can become so absorbed in our daily lives we forget about our relationships and let them fall to the wayside. We forget how much the other person means to us. It's unfortunate if they seem to become a responsibility along with everything else. What can we do to nourish our relationships when this occurs? What can we do to keep our awareness of all that's of value in our lives today? It's to our benefit to stop and think about this. What do we cherish? What do we love and cherish about this other person? What do we love and cherish about ourselves? Do we have a meaningful relationship? What we want may not be what we feel we are getting. What do we do then? Do we rock the boat? Or do we silently put up with what's occurring?

It's to our benefit to:

- Learn to speak up within our relationships.
- Tell the other person what we want and what we need.
- Learn to trust ourselves, to trust we are worth loving.
- Learn to give to another in a way that's beneficial to them.
- Learn to listen to each other. You may not always agree with your partner, but it's important you listen to and respect their point of view.
- To give and to receive. If our relationship goes only one way, we will soon lose the energy to maintain it.

What we want might be more than the person we are involved with is able to give. What do we do then? Do we look at our desires to see if they are realistic? What are you asking another person to do for you? Are there things you can do for yourself first? How do you know until you try? Try to be more loving and supportive of yourself. That's not solely the other person's job and responsibility; it's yours as well. Trust yourself, love yourself, and see what happens. Doing so will be of tremendous value to you and to any of the people in your life. Decide what you want. Be prepared to give yourself as much as you possibly can. Be willing also to reach out to this other person and offer what you can in the way of love and understanding. However, be careful to be honest and truthful in what you give to another. It would be dishonest to lead another to believe you have much more to give than you truly do.

Choose to base your relationship on *truth and integrity*. What better foundation can you build a relationship on? Do the best you can to have a deep and meaningful relationship with yourself as well as the other person. This will have a positive effect on the quality of your life and the lives around you

Love is so important to our lives. Most of us have wounds within ourselves to heal. We attract people who can help us heal these wounds, people who are unable to love us the way we want to be loved, forcing us to look elsewhere. Perhaps we should start looking within for what we want and need. It's helpful to become more conscious of the drives and desires we have and to examine why we choose to direct our energy to certain people who it may not be beneficial for us to invite into our lives. Look at your patterns; look at your life. What are you trying to teach yourself?

Must it all be about learning? Yes, to a certain degree, it's all about learning. What can we learn from each other? What do we teach? Don't deceive yourself by thinking you only teach. That's not the truth; the truth is we all have things to learn, and it's necessary to learn first of all to *humble* ourselves to this process of learning. If our egos and insecurities get the best of us, we will be unable to learn much of anything. Instead, we will repeat the same patterns over and over. The hard part is to be willing to be honest with ourselves, truthful to another, and vulnerable in many situations. This is the only way we will learn and grow. This is the only way we will be able to bring to ourselves a relationship of value.

Can you imagine how difficult it would be to learn from another person if you for some odd reason felt you had to have all the answers and be right all of the time? That's what we try to do at times. Try to let go of your defenses. Know within yourself you don't always know what is going on and what the solutions are to all problems. Be willing to humble yourself and say, "I just don't know." Be willing to allow another person to try to help you. Be willing to listen to what another has to say. You might find it extremely helpful. Begin to trust and to love yourself enough so you can be vulnerable to another's presence—to another's words.

Are you willing to put yourself in a vulnerable place to get what you want? If you aren't, you are limiting the communication and the sharing that can take place in your relationship. It's alright to be nervous and scared. You may be scared that the other person will leave you if they know who you really are. Try to let go of this fear because at the same time you are holding them at a distance, they are wondering why you find it necessary to do so. You are pushing them away anyway; it will just be a matter of time before they leave, so why not risk it and allow them closer?

Be willing to share your innermost self with another person. Don't feel you have to hide any aspect of your personality. We are all human. We all have things to learn. A relationship is a wonderful opportunity to learn more about ourselves and the people to whom we are attracted.

It's time to make the commitment to have more deeply intimate, more deeply honest relationships. It's only when we can do this that we will truly find happiness, love, and joy within ourselves and within the relationship we share with another.

CHAPTER 20

Accept What You Ask For

What do you want from another person? Are your needs reasonable? How can you tell if they are? Ask the person you want so much from if they are able or willing to give it to you. If they say no, what will you do then? You will be faced with making a decision. You will have to decide if what you say you want from another is really essential to your well-being. If it is, you might want to remove yourself from the relationship. If it isn't, you can try to stay with this person, provided you can release these needs or find some other avenue of fulfilling them.

What do we want and need from another? Usually it's what will make us feel good about ourselves. A lot of what we want and need from ourselves, we first try to get from another. It's only when that other person isn't available to us that we have to try to fulfill our own needs. Why aren't we first able to come to ourselves for these things? Because that isn't usually the pattern we develop as a child. If or when you needed something, who did you turn to? Was it a parent, or was it someone else? How many times were you able to fulfill your own needs? This pattern of turning to another was developed very early on in your life. It's not so easy to change this pattern. First, it's necessary to be conscious that it exists, and once you know it does, what are you going to do about it? You can decide whether what you need should come from another or whether it should come from you. Each time you make this choice, this decision, be prepared to accept what you ask for. Be willing to accept what you ask for or it will never be yours. You can ask time and time again, but if you close yourself off to receiving what you are asking for, how do you expect to receive it?

Many times we think we aren't loved because of the way we are in the world. This could be because of the way we act, the way we look, or our inability to be successful and stand out among others around us. Whether we are loved has a great deal to do with how we feel about ourselves. Beauty in looks and success in career aren't a true measure of worth, but a superficial standard set by some. *You are worth loving simply because you are.* Why do we find that so difficult to believe and to accept? How many times has someone tried to love you and you turned them away because you didn't feel deserving of the love they were trying to give? You might not think this applies to you, but if you pay close attention to all of the relationships in your life, you will notice how much you are willing to receive from those around you. How often are you offered material goods just to turn them away? How often are you offered help and assistance only to tell the person offering that you are just fine? Why do you do this? Why don't you simply feel open to receiving what another person offers?

A lot of the time we don't feel we deserve the help and the kindness others offer. Why don't we? What is wrong with us that we are unable to open our hands and accept what is being offered?

If you are still thinking, "I don't do this," watch the next time you're offered something. No matter what it is, try to be open to receiving it. Once you can be aware of what you say yes to and what you turn away, you will begin to see this pattern of self-sufficiency on a greater scale. Try to work on being more open to receiving the gifts and offerings others bring your way. The more you can do this, the fuller your life will be and the more you will have to share with those around you.

When we think of relationships, we tend to think only of couples. We have a relationship of some sort with each person we know. It's of benefit to us to expand our interpretation of what a relationship is. A relationship is any interaction with another human being or object. It's important to define and explore all our relationships and whether they are ones we want to keep, or if it's necessary to let them go. The more we can explore our relationships on a wider universal basis, the more we will allow others to enter and to leave our lives—and the less likely we will feel the compulsion to cling to each other. It's of value to develop more flexibility within the relationships we have with each other. There are things that are essential to maintaining a strong, healthy relationship with another person, but we want to really look at what we are asking and whether it's really necessary.

It's important we start loving ourselves and each other more fully. We do this by letting go of the fear that holds us back. Many times we are so afraid we will love another person, and they will leave us, that we choose to let them go before it's really time to do so. Why do we do this? Do we tell ourselves that it's the only way we can protect ourselves? Do you realize that at the same time you are protecting yourself, you are also putting your life on hold? You are distancing someone who might possibly be there to help you heal from the pain you already hold inside?

It's time to be more open to the love in our life. It's time to be willing to communicate with each other on a deeper level by sharing our pain with each other. Our goal is for us to communicate with each other all that we feel. Maybe what we want won't match up with what the person we love wants. What do we do then? We decide whether to stay in the relationship and try to work things out or whether it's necessary to let each other go. Occasionally, we let each other go before we have learned all that we can possibly learn. Why do we do this? Because we are afraid of loving and not having it turn out the way we want. Why can't we just love and let it turn out whatever way it does? Because we can't stand the uncertainty; we want to be in control and to know what is going to happen next. We want to know the other person will be there in our life whether or not it's to their benefit. We need so much from a relationship before it even begins that at times we are doomed from day one. How does a relationship survive all the needs we have? It's only when we can begin to release some of these needs—creating space for the other person to exist—that any of this can truly be worked out.

Even if you love yourself and try harder in a relationship to commit to working things out no matter what, you can't do this alone. Both people in a relationship have to commit. If one person commits and the other doesn't, then you will have a weak relationship. What can you do to make this other person commit? You can ask them, but if they refuse, then there is absolutely nothing you can do. You can only move forth in love for yourself. This doesn't mean you no longer love this other person, but it does mean you are limited in what you can share and experience within the relationship you have with them. Are you willing to settle for what you have? If you aren't, are you strong enough to do something about it?

The lessons are all about loving yourself. Do you see it? The more you can love yourself, the more you will be able to recognize that ability to love within another. You will then be able to draw to yourself someone with the same ability you possess to love and be loved. It may not seem that it always works out this way because each person in a relationship is so unique, but it does. You only attract to yourself what you yourself are able to give. It's not just a matter of giving; it's also a matter of being able to receive from another what they possess within themselves to share with you. Once you can do that more fully, you will be able to share your life with someone who is more capable of this also. If this is an area of your life that requires some work, please take the time to do it. The rewards are very fulfilling, for not only will the flow of love increase, but so will your awareness of the needs of another. You will be able to be present more fully in any and all of your relationships.

The love in your life will flow with greater ease and much less difficulty if you are open to *both giving and receiving*. What you give to another will come back to you many times over. Begin to do this work on yourself. Learn to not only give to another, but also to be more open to what another has to share with you.

To Give and to Receive

Unfortunately, some people treat relationships as if they hold little importance. Who do these people turn to when they need a friend? Who do these people turn to when times get hard?

We don't always pay enough attention to our relationships. What do we expect from others and what are we ready to give? We might expect a great deal—and might be ready to give very little. Why do we think we should receive so much when we can give so little ourselves? It could be your mother or your father showered you with love and attention and didn't ask much of you in return.

Look at the relationship you had with your parents. Could that be a reflection of the way you expect to be in other relationships?

To be in a relationship requires you to be able to think of someone besides yourself. In order to do this, you must be able to detach enough from your life to look around and see other people. Be aware—your friends, your family, your partner, or whoever may also be in a place of being challenged by their life. It's when we can see the challenges present for others that we can begin to participate from a level of *heart-to-heart interaction* that will further deepen and solidify the relationships we have. If we think only of ourselves, we will lose out on many opportunities to have the type of relationship we would cherish.

Many people are raised to have independent attitudes, which can interfere with their ability to reach out to others or to ask for help. Why are we so afraid to ask for help? Does it mean we are of lesser value because we need help? Does it mean we have failed in some way? Why are we so harsh and demanding of ourselves? We might want to look at our expectations and do a little soul searching. It's important to be able to reach out and help others, but we also need to be open to receiving and possibly asking for help for ourselves. This can be a very humbling experience. It can feel like we aren't able to care for ourselves. Sometimes life puts us in this situation so we can learn to open our hearts to ourselves, as well as to others who eventually find themselves in the same situation.

When you can detach and trust that somehow you will work your way through this experience, you will be able to be present with the people you love in a more loving way. When life presents great challenges for us, our tendency can be to separate and move away from the ones who are really able to give us the most love and support. Something inside of us might be telling us we aren't worthy of someone's caring at this time. We may also be overwhelmed by the fact we aren't in control of everything that happens in our lives.

Do your relationships fall apart because you find yourself unworthy of this love and support, or do they serve to help you through this time of challenge? Your experience will have a lot to do with what you are able and willing to accept from those around you. If you can detach enough not to judge yourself, you will be able to accept whatever love and support is there for you. If you can't do this, you might choose to destroy some of your best relationships because you can't bear to live with what's happening in your life. What are you going to do then, when you find yourself all alone? Perhaps you think it will be easier then because there won't be anyone around to witness the failure that you are. Why do you want to do this to yourself? Do you realize this is a choice you are making? Do you realize there are other choices?

When times get difficult, if we can work on increasing the love we show ourselves, we will have so much more balance and stability in our life. We will be able to share this balance and stability with those we love. If possible, try not to withdraw. You might want some time for yourself, but try hard not to pull away from those you love. When we pull away, we strain the strings that attach us. Sometimes these strings become so stretched and strained we aren't able to keep our relationships. Do be conscious of the choices you are making at this time. What is the most loving thing you can do for yourself? It's time to do it, to open yourself to communicating your thoughts and feelings and to accepting the help you need.

Loving is what being in and having a relationship is all about. It's about loving and honoring yourself, it's about *sharing* your gifts with another, and it's about *receiving* what another has to share. Open yourself to this very enlightening

experience. Open yourself to feeling the love that exists within your own being. It all starts with you.

CHAPTER 21
Listening to What Another Has to Tell Us

Gaining awareness of how other people react to us and to our behavior gives us a great deal of information. At times we can get caught up in thinking only of ourselves and our own needs. It's imperative to think of others and their needs as well. In order to do this, we have to really hear what another person is telling us. Perhaps they are not telling us what we think is important, but that's not the issue. It's what they think is important that must be considered at this time. Don't judge it, just listen to it and whether we agree with it or not, realize that it's valuable information someone has shared with us.

Valuing Another Person's Words

It's important to realize the value in every human being with whom we share each day. We are all of great value. We all deserve to be treated with respect. We do this by:

- Listening to what others tell us.
- Really hearing what they say.
- Not changing what they say into what suits and benefits us.
- Not later using their words as ammunition against them.

In order to have a strong relationship, we must learn how to communicate effectively with each other. We have so much to learn, if only we can be more open to this process of learning and not take everything so personally. We so easily take the words of another as an attack against our value. What another has to say to us has nothing to do with our value or our worthiness as far as being a human worth loving, but it does have to do with our behavior and actions in this world of interactions with others. We all have things to learn in this department. Every one of us would benefit from the kind words of another telling us what we are doing that they find challenging to live with or to experience as a friend.

The Difference in Being Attacked or Talked to by Someone

Be willing to listen to what others have to say. Use their words as an opportunity to learn more about yourself. Go within to decide if what they say is true. Are they striking out at you, or are they truly trying to tell you something of value for you to hear? A big difference exists between being attacked and being talked to by someone. Distinguishing between the two will aid you in your life. To be attacked is to be hurt and injured by someone you love. To be talked to is to have someone who cares tell you what their needs are. At times, we fail to distinguish between these two ways of sharing information. Attacks are never growth oriented; talks are. We want to learn to talk to each other and to receive the words of another without injuring ourselves because we then perceive ourselves to be of less value. Our value isn't what is being questioned; it's our behavior. But often we aren't able to distinguish between these two. It's time to learn to communicate with each other. It's time we stop taking offense at anything and everything our partner says to us. Stop reacting and instead allow yourself to be vulnerable and listen to the words that are really being said. When we can begin to do this, we can begin to have a relationship that's built on the trust and the love we have for ourselves. This will be the strongest relationship of all. We can share so much of ourselves with another person when we can trust that we are worth loving regardless of what another person could say to us. It takes a certain level of detachment to work from this base, but the more you can trust and love yourself, the easier it will be to detach.

It's time to listen to what your friends tell you. It's time to let the people you love know the truth. Let's try to open up to each other more every day. The more we can do this, the more we will have a life and a community in which we want to live. What must we do to have this? We need to be able to listen to *what another person has to tell us*. We have to be able to step back and hear their words, knowing it's not an attack on us as a person, but information that will help us to do what we can to become more compatible with those around us. We don't always have to make changes because of what another says, but at times we can see the truth in their words and realize it would be to our benefit to do so.

Realizing the Information Is for Our Awareness

It's essential we detach from the information we are given. It's not done to bring us pain; it's there for our awareness, to make us aware of what we are doing and how it's affecting the people around us. We can listen, then we can decide for ourselves what changes should be made. Perhaps we want to change a great deal about ourselves, and we feel overwhelmed by it. It could be we have little to change, but we have the challenge of telling someone we care for what it is about their behavior that challenges us. All you can do is tell them, and then you have to let it go. Don't expect them to embrace what you say. Don't expect them to change because you have told them what's difficult about being with them. Don't expect anything; expect only that now you have done what you needed to do.

When we bring another person into our life, we want, in some way or another, to control our interaction with them. This behavior is natural up to a point. When our desire to control another gets out of hand, we will find ourselves making one ultimatum after another, and it will be doing us no good at all. When we find ourselves in this position, it might be a good idea to reconsider what you think you want from this person. Is what you want realistic? Are you expecting too much? What are your needs? What are their needs? Is it possible for both people to have their needs met within this relationship? If not, what are you going to do? Can you surrender your needs? If you do, what will happen to your happiness within this relationship? You have a lot of things to consider.

When we find ourselves in a relationship that's overly challenging, how do we deal with it? Do we communicate our needs to the other person? Do we listen to what they tell us, or do we just pretend we do? Pretending to hear another means you do actually hear the words, but then you dismiss them as unimportant and continue on your way. You have no idea how often you do this. How can I tell when I am doing this? You can tell by paying attention to the other person's reaction. Have they reached a point where they don't even want to talk about it because it seems to do no good? The resurfacing of the same issues is a good indication that the words are being spoken, but you aren't really hearing them, and you aren't honoring the value of their words and the meaning they hold for the person speaking them. *It's easy to brush off the words of another as having little to no value if they aren't what we believe is the truth of the situation.*

What we don't realize is that we decide that our interpretation of the situation is the only one that exists. *It's what we think that's important.* We are really *not honoring* what the other person is telling us. We can't get past the belief that because we think what we do, they must be wrong. It isn't a matter of being right or wrong. It's a matter of you experiencing one thing—and your partner or friend experiencing another. Both experiences should be acknowledged, honored, and taken into consideration for a relationship to have two people in it that feel heard. It's *very important to hear and to be heard.* It's essential to the health of a relationship. If one isn't heard, soon one stops speaking and becomes silent. Soon one stops participating in the communication that needs to take place in a healthy relationship. What do you want for yourself? Do you want to always be right and always be in control, or do you want to listen and learn from what another tells you?

To Compromise, We Have to Be Able to Really Hear What Another Tells Us

What does the word *compromise* mean? Does it mean you never get what you want because someone else's needs always seem to take priority? Or does it mean you share and take turns getting your needs met? Look carefully at the word *compromise.* What does it mean to you? Do you know how to take turns? Frequently we think we share a lot with others because we give them what we believe they need—when what they really want and need has nothing to do with what we are offering them. Do you wonder why relationships often don't work? It's because we haven't fully developed the skill of *listening* to each other. Once we can do this, it will solve a great many difficulties that arise.

What do you hear when someone tells you what they want? Do you listen closely, or do you think you know what they are going to say? Frequently you misinterpret, causing you to jump to the wrong conclusions. When this occurs, what do you do? Do you defend yourself by saying, "But you always do that!" or "I know what you are really thinking." Practice letting go of your thoughts and let them tell you what they think and want. Try not to assume anything. You might think you know this person so well, but that might not be the truth. We are all ever-changing human beings. No matter how long you have been with someone, things do change within people and in their way of thinking about things.

Questions to ponder:

- What am I willing to do for the sake of my relationship?
- Am I willing to change some of my ways?
- Am I willing to try to be a better listener?
- Am I willing to respect another person's wants and needs even if I don't understand and can't relate to them?

What is damaging is to tell someone you love them yet be unwilling to listen to what they want. Each person's wants and needs vary. Realize what they are asking for is of great importance to them. Possibly we are programmed to give them one thing, and what they are asking for is something else. Are we going to stay with our program because that's what we were taught was important, or are we going to let go and make some changes in the way we choose to interact with those we love?

You will work your way through it, just listen carefully to what others ask of you. Don't feel you have to do something that goes against what you believe in to please another. The objective is *listening* and *really hearing* what another person tells you. This isn't about completely surrendering your whole self to someone else.

However, there is a balance to be maintained in being true to you, yet sharing yourself with others.

Listen to what another tells you. Realize this information is of *great value* in understanding this person. Be patient with yourself and with the person with whom you are learning to have this open communication. Learning to do this will improve all the relationships in your life.

SECTION 5
LEAVING A
RELATIONSHIP

CHAPTER 22
Do We Leave—or Do We Stay?

The relationship we are in may be special in many ways. There might be things about the person you cherish—but also things you don't like. What do you do when the things you care about in that person get lost in the things you don't like? You can choose to let go and allow them to leave your life, or you can put some effort and energy into trying to focus more clearly on what you like and love about them. We tend to get what we focus on, so be careful what you choose.

Ask yourself:

- Do I think I need to like the person I live with?
- What if there is a mixture of both qualities in the person. What do I do?
- Do I stay with this person because they are someone who is at least familiar to me?
- Do I stay because I'm not unhappy enough to leave?
- What is unhappy enough?

- Where do I draw the line? That's a difficult decision for anyone who sits on the fence about whether to stay in a relationship.
- What will be the deciding factor? What will push me off the fence one way or another?

Maybe the person's affection will pull you back to their side. But possibly their behavior—or lack of affection—will push you off the fence altogether. All you can do is wait until it feels right for you to stay or to leave.

We must take the time we need in leaving a relationship. We often rush out of a relationship only to find that later we regret the decision we have made. It's time to start making some conscious decisions. If you are making your decision out of anger, it's not a good time to be deciding. Wait until the anger has left, then if you can still decide to do what you originally intended, you will at least be proceeding from more stable ground.

Try to be kind and compassionate with each other. When we do decide to leave a relationship, we want to be willing to leave it with as much respect and regard for the other person as we possibly can. It's only by leaving in this manner that we will truly be able to be free of them. If you leave in anger and frustration, a chance exists that the person you leave will not be able to handle the choice you made. What we fail to realize is that all this amounts to is two people who once cared a great deal for each other choosing to hurt each other in every conceivable way. Is this really what you want? Is this really what you want to experience yourself?

It can be life changing if we choose to be conscious of how we leave each other. How we treat each person in our life makes a tremendous difference in the quality of the life we will lead. We might think what happens to us has nothing to do with our behavior in the world. This isn't always true. We have to start taking responsibility for ourselves and the way we treat others. When we are in a relationship, we can be truly challenged to stay respectful toward the other person. It's imperative we do. Without respect, what kind of relationship do you have? What are you doing to your relationship when you treat the person in your life that's closest to you with less respect than you would someone else? Really look at what you are doing to yourself and to the person you are pretending to love and respect. What is a relationship without love and respect? This love and respect needs to come forth from you, not just to you from the other person. The deterioration of love and respect shown to each other can be the downfall of your relationship.

When We Try to Leave a Relationship, but Something Pulls Us Back

Why did we leave in the first place? Did we feel something was missing? What was our motivation? Have things really changed, or have we decided to rethink our decision? Many things affect what we choose to do. We make many decisions that are changed or reversed only because of something that has happened since we made the first choice. We must decide what is best for us. If there are children involved, we might think we are making the choice because of them. They may indeed be a factor, but the ultimate choice comes down to what you can really live with and accept? Do be true to yourself so you can teach your children to do the same thing. Feel deep within your heart for the choice that will be in the best interests of everyone involved. That choice will be for your benefit because it will be the choice that will bring you the most peace.

When we choose to leave someone, other people can be affected by this choice because when we leave, we may also be leaving behind friends. We will be keeping friends as well, but even those people might relate to us differently. We want to prepare ourselves for the chain reaction of what our decision may have put into play. A lot will change about our life when we leave someone we have been close to for quite some time. One step at a time we can do this. It might take a while for us to get fully on our feet and functioning in a joyful mode, but it will come if we are prepared to take care of ourselves along the way.

At first you might need to work harder than ever to help yourself through the initial adjustment. Be sure to take time to give yourself breaks and treats along the way. When we learn to love and nourish ourselves, we won't miss the absence of someone else we had so hoped would do these things for us.

Build a life of love. The only way you can do this is by being the most loving human being you can possibly be. *Open your heart* and do this now. Do it for you and do it for all the people in the world who could use a little more love and a little more light.

CHAPTER 23

Loving Yourself as You "Let Go"

Trust and love yourself, and be willing to let go of all that's no longer necessary to your life and to your happiness. This could mean letting go of a great deal. What are you prepared to release? What do you feel is essential to keep in your life? This will be a process of loving and letting go.

How many of us know how to love another person and yet let them go when the time is right? How do we know when the time is right? The time that's right for them may not feel right for us. What do we do when we find ourselves in this situation? Do we get angry at them for not loving us enough? Do we get angry and try to hurt them, or do we simply let them go? How do we get to this place of letting go where we no longer feel we want to inflict pain upon another? We get there by loving ourselves and knowing we are of great value regardless of what another person chooses for themselves.

What can we do for ourselves when we feel the pain of being left by someone we love? We can love ourselves. Loving ourselves isn't a lofty ideal; it's a moment by moment, day by day way of treating yourself.

Ask yourself:

- What do I do to take care of myself when I feel down?
- What do I do to bring myself back up?
- What messages do I give myself?
- Am I creating more pain because of the messages I am giving myself?
- How am I *choosing to perceive* this situation?
- Can I change my perception so it gives me more support?
- What can I say to myself to make it better?
- What can I learn?

How we treat ourselves is about learning and also about loving. Frequently we think about love only in terms of how we reach out and touch another. It's time we thought of it in terms of how we treat ourselves. We need to be loving, kind, and generous with ourselves. It's only when we do this that we will really feel the love we all hold within. We need to reach out to ourselves as we would reach out to our best friend. Let go of all the negative messages. Yes, you are good enough to be loved; you just need to do it for yourself in this moment.

Many times we push ourselves aside, thinking it doesn't matter what happens to us. It does matter. If we don't matter to ourselves, how can we expect to matter to someone else? What do you think? What do you feel? That matters and is important. Share what you think and feel with those around you. Perhaps you choose only to share with a select few. That's alright if you find you get enough support for yourself this way. It's important you find a way to love and support yourself. Friends are important at times like this. Perhaps you are short on friends. If that's true, it's never too late to reach out to someone and make them your friend. We might choose to hold so much inside because we can't imagine that anyone else can understand our situation—our pain. What we tend to do then is to alienate ourselves and further isolate ourselves from living a life of fullness. It all depends on what you feel that you need for yourself. This is what you want to honor. Honor what you feel.

What if you feel a great deal of anger? Do you act on it? What do you hope to achieve if you do? Perhaps you think it will make you feel better to strike out and hurt another. Maybe you don't quite understand that what you do to another, you in essence do to yourself. This effect is important to understand. Somehow, in some way, what we have done to another will come back to us. What do you want for yourself? Think about that before you reach out to do harm to anyone else. Pretend you are holding a mirror and everything you put out is reflected right back at you. Don't put yourself in the situation of having to experience anything other than what you would want to experience.

It's time we all learn to deal with our anger. It's a very strong, *natural* emotion. It can warn us that we are being taken advantage of in some way. It's important to look at why these feelings of anger are accumulating. If you can pay close attention and call it by its name, the anger you are beginning to feel will be dissipated in no time. It's when you don't pay attention to it, and then find yourself consumed by this particular emotion, that you run the risk of losing control of yourself. Pay attention. Choose to call it by its name as soon as you feel the beginning of it starting. Think of it as clouds gathering before a storm. If you can identify the clouds as "anger" before too many of them accumulate, you can minimize the effects and the outcome of the storm. As children, we aren't always taught how to deal with our feelings; then, as adults, we continue on in the same way we did as a child. Do you want to do this? How do you choose to deal with your anger and frustration? Do you choose to take it out on whoever is around you, or do you remove yourself from the situation and then try to find an outlet that will help you release this pent-up frustration? What do you do? Do you realize it's never too late to change your behavior? All you have to do is be aware of your behavior and watch as the situation presents itself, allowing you to consciously choose how you are going to deal with it. This can be a tremendously rewarding experience. To deal with your anger, to identify it before it becomes too late, is quite a challenge at first, but it will have a lasting positive effect on your life and the lives of those around you.

Love yourself, trust your life. Take the time to be patient with yourself. Give yourself the most positive, honest messages you possibly can. This can take some time and effort on your part, and from time to time you may fall back into old patterns, but be determined to make the necessary changes so you can have the best life possible. You aren't doing this just for yourself, you're also doing it for everyone who is in your life and who may possibly enter your life at any future date. It's necessary to love and care for ourselves before we can truly do it for another. Take the time to do this. Treat yourself as if you are the most special person in the world. This doesn't mean you are any more important than anyone else, but it does mean you are important, you are special, and you are divine. This should be celebrated. You want to be able to see and recognize the beauty of your own spirit. When you can do that, you will see much more beauty reflected in the world around you. These aren't just words; this is *a way of living*, a way of loving yourself and those around you. Have the courage to embrace yourself and those you love. Trust yourself. Be kind. Take the time you need to heal before entering into another relationship. Take the time to become your own best friend. You will notice a significant change in your life when you do this.

Be honest, be truthful. Share what you think, feel, and want. Let another know you for who you really are. If they choose not to be with you, then realize it was for the best. They may choose to leave you, but as long as you don't choose to leave yourself, you will be just fine.

Maybe what you truly need is time to come to know and understand yourself better. We don't always have to do things in pairs. We can learn so much about life by being on our own. It's too bad if we think we have to have another person in our life to truly be fulfilled. Once we can live on our own and meet our own needs, we will have more of ourselves to share with another when we do enter into a relationship.

Wait for the person that's right for you. Trust they are out there somewhere. It doesn't mean you will necessarily meet them when you want to; you may have to wait for some time. What is most important: to be with a person you truly love, or to have just anyone by your side? True love is possible. Realize this truth within yourself so you can experience it with another. Begin to feel this love within—and begin to understand that eventually you can have what you want if you are willing to wait long enough. This waiting takes patience. What do you want to learn about in the meantime? Do you want to learn to love and trust yourself, or do you want to hang your head in sorrow because you don't have anyone to love you the way you know you deserve to be loved? You decide.

Pay attention, trust, detach, and love. That's all you can do, and make the best possible choices you can. Love yourself, be kind, be gentle, be patient, and be understanding.

When you can do all of this for yourself, your life will be very full indeed.

CHAPTER 24
How We Leave Each Other?

Be aware of how you choose to let go of someone. Are you afraid of hurting them? If you are, what do you do to make it easier for them to understand your position? It's to our benefit to start looking at our friendships, intimate and otherwise. How do we choose to leave each other? Is it with kind words? What do we say to this person who has been our friend for so long—and possibly much more than that? Do we treat them with respect? Do we trust them enough to share our innermost thoughts and feelings? If we don't, why is that? What can we do to improve the quality of the relationships we have? We can begin by treating each other with more kindness and love.

Why is it necessary to be loving with someone we are leaving? Because it's important how you treat another person. If you are leaving in anger, it might be quite impossible to do this. If it's too difficult to leave on good terms, then try not to compound and complicate everything even more by adding abuse from your side of the situation. If you have a hard time refraining from fighting back, ask yourself if you would really like to experience what you are determined to put the other person through. If your answer is no—please don't do it. We have to stop the pain and anguish somewhere. Be the strong one; be the one that says, "No, that doesn't feel good. No, I consciously choose not to inflict any further pain on anyone else in my life."

Every so often we leave relationships thinking our behavior won't matter. After all, we won't be seeing this person anymore, and even if we are, they don't mean anything to us. Do you realize how self-centered and self-serving this thought is? Who are you thinking of? Yourself alone—certainly not the other person. Why is it so difficult to think about them? Yes, you might be in pain, and it may be pain that came forth from a situation created by them, but does that really give you an excuse to injure and harm another person?

It's important we release our compulsion to seek revenge upon someone who doesn't live up to our expectations. It can make such a difference in our lives if we can learn how to let go of relationships without having to thoroughly trash them first. Why can't we state what we feel, set our boundaries, and let the other person move on? Why do we have to be destructive to them and to ourselves? It's beneficial for us to look at how we act and behave in a relationship and also at the end of one. It's time to change some of the patterns we have developed in relating to each other. Changing these patterns can help us to heal our pain and differences. We can't do this if we are always creating more. If we can learn to trust ourselves and let the other person go, we will truly be free to live our lives from our heart. Letting go in a non-abusive way is very important. Try it, and you will experience the benefits.

The next time you decide to end a relationship, try to do it in a way that's beneficial to both people involved. This could be a challenge to do, but it will certainly be a worthwhile one. When you are finally able to do this, you will be reminded of all the love in the world. You will no longer be focused on the pain and the hurt. It's important to learn how to do this. It's important for your well-being as well as for all who surround you. Every relationship in your life has a beginning and an ending. Do you really want to end every relationship in pain and hurt, or do you want to be able to reach out to another with kindness? When you reach out to another with kindness, both people in the relationship feel and experience the effects. Why can't you decide to end your present relationships in love? This might be beyond your comprehension at this time, but if you try with each relationship to be as honest and supportive of yourself and of the other person as you can, you will soon come to a place of knowing how to do this. It's helpful to take it one step at a time. No giant steps, for they will only leave you with a lot of unfinished business. Learning to leave your relationships with kindness in your heart—but also being clear about what you feel you didn't get—is a time of considerable learning for everyone.

What if you didn't have the kind of relationship where communication was involved? How can one not communicate with someone with whom they are involved? They can "not" communicate by never really speaking up about what they are thinking and feeling. Not speaking up is really not so uncommon. We might think we are participating in a mutual relationship only to find later that we were the only one talking. What do we do then? Do we decide to further complicate the situation by demanding the other person tell us what they want, or do we simply move on to someone else? Each person will decide for themselves how they want to leave a relationship. You can leave it with kindness in your heart, but unless all your issues have been resolved within you, you won't have much peace from the situation. What happens when things arise later that challenge you? Do you call that person on the phone and tell them off, or do you choose to let it go? This too will be different for each person. What we choose to do for ourselves will vary. For some people, it will be better to simply let go. They know deep in their hearts nothing can be achieved by remaining in the present situation—or by trying to further communicate with the person they left.

You can decide for yourself what is most important for you to do. Follow your innermost guidance. When you do this, you will be watching out for what is in your own best interest. If you choose to go against your clearest instincts, you will have an opportunity to learn from that also. What do you want for yourself? Be willing to look at your true motives for any actions you take—or fail to take. It's easy to get into an "I'll show them" attitude. This will only bring harm to both people involved and possibly others as well.

Decide how you can best take care of yourself and continue on with your life. Don't keep looking back. The time to understand what occurred could be long gone. What is important are your present moments. You want to continue living your life in a way that nurtures, loves, and supports you. Once you are more able to do this, the transition from being in a relationship to being on your own will come with greater ease.

Detach, trust, and let go over and over again. This is a good time to practice detaching from your present situation. Don't let it define you. Don't let it control you. Detach from it and focus on the good/wonderful life you will create for yourself. You still need to feel and to release your pain, but at the same time you are doing that, it's also possible to do things for yourself that say, "I care, I am worth the love I feel for myself." In doing this self-care, you will be able to heal and move forth into life from a much more positive place.

Trust yourself, take good care of yourself, and be willing to let the other person go—he or she isn't essential to your life. You will have a life regardless of what the other person does or doesn't do. It's beneficial to realize that the quality of your life depends solely upon you and what you decide to do for yourself. You can take care of yourself and build a good life, or you can abuse yourself and make yourself suffer for the loss you incurred. It's up to you. Did you realize you do have a choice—and that the choice you make will influence and design your future for you?

To create the best future:

- Begin to love and support yourself more.
- Trust yourself and the choices you make.
- Know and understand there's not always one right answer; sometimes there are many right answers that take your life in different directions.
- Pick yourself up, brush yourself off, and get on with living your life.

Yes, you can grieve, but don't lose yourself in grief. Don't forget who is creating the experience of your life: you are. Stand up and take responsibility for it. Make it the best life you can. Love yourself, trust yourself, and be kind to yourself. Do what you can to love and support yourself through this time of change and transition. It will be beneficial to you and to everyone else in your life.

Take the time to do this work. It's called *the work of loving and letting go.* **You love yourself as best you can; you let go of your former relationship and move on into your own life. Create this life for yourself. Make it beautiful. Fill it with all the things you love the most.**

SECTION 6
THE WORK OF RELATIONSHIPS

CHAPTER 25
Opening to Growth

Relationships are powerful tools for growth and learning if we can allow ourselves to approach our conflicts with that perspective. "What can I learn from this experience?" is what you need to be willing to ask yourself. Once you can do that, you are opening up to an understanding even greater than what you presently own. You are acknowledging you aren't perfect—that perhaps you can learn something from what occurs in your life. If the person you are in a relationship with can adopt this same perspective, it means two people are relating to each other who are open to learning and growing from their life experiences. This opening to growth is so important. It teaches us not only what we have to learn; it allows us to do it in a more supportive environment. Yes, there will still be anger and frustration. Yes, the other person may still pull away from you from time to time, but what you will have is a relationship built on trust because both people know the *main objective* isn't to win the argument, but to learn and to grow from it. If both people are true in their hearts about using this process of growth from inner conflict, then it will also be a great source of support for their relationship.

Important "We Need" Points.

We need to really:

- Look at what we want from the other person.
- Be aware of the pitfalls of a relationship.
- Be willing and able to learn from our mistakes and from the pain we may be bringing to another person.
- Be willing to be open to experiencing our own pain as well.

Only when we can do this will we be able to release our pain, to let it go. When we let this pain go, we can feel more love for ourselves and for others. We all have pain to release. The work of being in a relationship is about getting in touch with this pain and letting it go. Don't hold on to your pain; choose to release it, to let it go.

How do you let your pain go? You simply feel it and let it go. For a time, it may not seem like it has really left you. Often there's a great deal of buried pain that can only be experienced and released a little at a time. It's alright to take the time for yourself to feel and release this pain. When you do take this time, however, make sure you do it with respect to this person who is so close to you. Tell them what you are doing and why. Don't leave them in the dark to figure out why you have temporarily left them alone. Be kind to each other. We don't want to create more pain, but we want to release our pain and do it with respect to the person with whom we may be sharing our life. This mutual respect while we hold space for each other to release our pain creates a bond that heals both people.

How to Learn from Our Relationships:

Don't look back to the past, don't look ahead to the future, be right where you are in this moment. Be with who you are with today, right now—it's all that matters. If you can be fully present with the person you love, you will have more of yourself to share with them. They need your love and also your attention. Frequently we are too busy to really pay attention to each other. What kind of a relationship do you want for yourself? Do you want one where both you and your partner basically live together, not sharing much but the space you live in? If you are satisfied with that, then that's what you will get. If you aren't, you might try to talk to your partner to see if they will agree to slow their life down so the two of you can have more time together.

It takes having time together to allow two people to share their thoughts and feelings with each other. If there's no time together, there will also be no sharing of thoughts and feelings. What do you want? Do you want a truly intimate relationship, or do you merely want to live with someone you barely know? You might think you know them well because you have lived with them for so long, but you have no idea what is really going on in their mind. How frequently do you hear married people say, "And I thought I knew him so well?" We think we know each other, but we don't. It's impossible to know what another person is thinking. There may be times when you can seem to read each other's thoughts, but other times when you have no idea what the person is thinking or feeling. It's only by taking the time to share with each other that we will have a relationship that will grow over time and always be fresh and new. It also takes being willing to work daily to remove any blocks that come between ourselves and the other person. It's only by clearing away these blockages that we can share what we feel.

Commit yourself to doing all that's in your power to hold your relationship together. At times it will be difficult, if not impossible, to share your thoughts with each other. When this occurs, give each other the time and space to work things out. Don't grasp at each other. Don't hold each other so tightly there isn't room to breathe. Let the other person go; let them have time to come to whatever realizations are there for them.

In some relationships, one person is willing to give so much more than the other person. What happens when this occurs is a critical imbalance in the relationship. The two people may not even be aware this is happening. In time, however, one person will find it unbearable to continue with things the way they are because they aren't getting their needs met. When this occurs, a buildup of anger and frustration can be present. To diminish this anger and frustration, the person must realize the part they play. First of all, no one makes you do anything. If you do anything, it's because you have decided to do it. You have decided to participate on some level of your being. There is the potential to learn from the imbalance in your relationship. The lesson might be to walk away from the relationship and take good care of yourself. Can you do that? The lesson could also be about learning to communicate your thoughts and feelings. You might be surprised by the other person's reactions if you clearly speak up about what you want and feel.

Often we think the other person should know what we think and feel without us saying a word. Do you realize how ridiculous this expectation is? It's merely an excuse you can use not to take responsibility for speaking up about what you think, want, and need. Until you can begin to speak up, you are asking more from your partner than they may be able to give. You are asking them to know and to accept what little of yourself you are willing to share. Frequently people ask this of each other because they are afraid that if this other person really knew them, they would leave. You might want to look at why you think so little of yourself.

It's time we all begin to pay more attention to what is happening in our lives. Sometimes we have the grandest of plans, but our life doesn't seem to go that way no matter what we do. There is such a thing as *surrender* when this occurs. To surrender doesn't mean we give up on ourselves and our life, but it means we surrender to what is presently occurring. It means we have awareness, but we acknowledge we aren't always the one in control. We can't control everything that happens. Wait and see what occurs in your life; take notice of how much control you really have. You might have to let go of things, ideas, or people you had no intention of releasing.

It seems a lot is going on right now in the lives of all people—both challenges and amazing things. What do you choose to focus on? What does your partner choose to focus on? Be careful what you focus on, for that's the direction you will move. Try to perceive your life in the most positive way you possibly can. When you do this for yourself, you bring energy into your life and into the lives of those around you. Enhancing everyone's energy is a gift. It can be hard to pull ourselves up and out of the difficult times. At times we pass judgments on ourselves that really aren't necessary. Kindness and compassion are of paramount importance. The world is greatly challenged. How we think and feel about each other matters. At times like this, it's our relationships with each other that can be our greatest source of comfort and pleasure.

Detach from what occurs in your life. Trust everything that happens. Make the best of your life that you can. Let go of all that isn't important.

Tell yourself that whatever you are now experiencing is just passing through. That doesn't mean you don't need to take responsibility for your thoughts and your actions but it does mean you acknowledge the *impermanence* of all things.

CHAPTER 26

Sharing Our
Innermost Thoughts

It's time we share our innermost thoughts with each other. It will bring us to a deeper level of sensitivity and understanding. Isn't this what we want? To be able to relate to each other in the most intimate way? Though you might be challenged by this, it's time to trust yourself more. Be willing to share what you think and feel with your partner. If you can't share it with them, who can you share it with? It could be you have a friend you share your most intimate thoughts with, and you save your physical relationship for your partner. Sure, it's difficult if not impossible to depend on one person to have all your needs met, but this isn't about getting all your needs met by one person; it's about sharing your innermost self with the person you love. What do you share with each other if you don't share your innermost thoughts? What makes you care about each other? What is most precious to you about the other person? Be aware of what it is and then be willing to tell them. It's time we confide in each other on a deeper level.

It's time to trust yourself. Trust that what you want and what you know about life is important. You have a right to share what you think and what you know with another. Don't be afraid you will embarrass yourself. Be kind to yourself, trust yourself and wrap yourself with arms of compassion. Know what you are attempting to do can be extremely challenging. You are opening yourself to another. You are exposing the most vulnerable aspect of yourself. Huge benefits will come from this manner of relating to each other.

You may be surprised at how beautiful your inner being is. You might be surprised at how close you feel to your partner when you share from a place of truth and inner knowing. It's only by being true to yourself that you will really know if the other person loves you for who you truly are—or for who you pretend to be. *Let yourself be known for who you really are.* This type of honesty is a lot of work. It will be very difficult at times. There will be times when you will be afraid you won't be accepted or understood. There may even be those times when you aren't accepted or understood. When this happens, don't abandon yourself. Love yourself back to wholeness; love yourself back to a stable place of being. You can do this. It might be a challenge to begin with, but once you start doing it, it will get easier. Be patient with yourself. Be determined to be your own best friend by trusting and loving yourself each step of the way.

Once you start to love yourself completely, you will be able to listen to what others have to say to you without feeling so threatened. Why would you feel threatened? When other people tell us we do or say things they don't like, we think what they are telling us is that they don't like us; they don't think we are worth loving. We have to be careful to listen to what is really being said. Once it's said, we want to be honest with ourselves as to whether it's something for us to own up to and be willing to change, or whether it's something we, really deep in our heart, don't believe relates to us.

What does it take to have a relationship where you can openly and honestly share with your partner? It takes a relationship where both people are willing to love and support each other while they love and support themselves. How do you do this when you tend to be pulling away from each other at that time? There are ways to pull away from each other—ways to disagree with each other, yet still treat each other with the respect needed because it's a stressful situation. You can disagree, yet respect the person. However, one important factor is your ability and willingness to really listen and hear the other person's viewpoint.

We can get so convinced we are right that we never really allow ourselves to hear what the other person says. Our work is to listen and respond to them with their own words, letting them know we hear what they say, and then share in all honesty what we feel. This is a complex situation that can be handled in a delicate, responsible manner if both people involved are willing to *consciously* do this work. It's the consciousness with which both people participate that will determine the outcome. You may come to a place where you both agree with each other, but you might also come to a place where you decide to respect each other's varied viewpoints. Whatever the conclusion, *most important* is how you treat each other throughout the process of resolving this conflict.

Why are we rarely taught to resolve conflict in a mutually supportive way? It might be because the people who raised you weren't quite able to achieve that themselves. It doesn't mean you can't. Being aware of the process of growth and change that needs to take place in your life, it's important to be careful in choosing a partner. It will be quite difficult to do this work of mutually supporting each other if you have a partner who isn't willing to participate in this manner. What can you do if you already have someone who isn't willing to do this work? You will have to continue on your own, but instead of experiencing the union that will come from this feeling of mutual support, you will have to make yourself content with the feelings of love and support you can give to yourself. It will be a different experience, but it will be worthwhile.

Our Ability to Communicate

What does communication mean to you? Perhaps it means telling someone what kind of a day you had. Some people limit their communication to the details of their day. Are you willing to settle for this? Is this what you want your relationship to be made of, the details of every day? What more is there? There is the value of your very being as well as the thoughts you think and the feelings you have—challenges present themselves and questions arise. There are the struggles you feel within your very soul. Yes, this all sounds so intriguing. It isn't so intriguing; it's everyday stuff, but it's everyday stuff we would only share with someone we really trusted, and then only if they took the time to listen and to care. So then what does that mean we want and need from a relationship? Possibly two people who can trust each other with what we hold most valuable inside, our innermost thoughts and feelings. Do you have this level of trust within the context of your relationship? If you do, that's absolutely wonderful.

If you don't, you might ask yourself why not:

- Why am I unable to share my most intimate self with the person I love?
- What have they done to prove to me that I must hold all of this inside, or possibly share it only with other people who can be trusted more than my partner?

- What happened to damage my relationship?
- Is there any hope it can be healed?
- Could the reason I am unable to share deep, intimate things have to do with my own inability to be open and sharing?
- What keeps me from doing this?
- What am I afraid of?
- What dark secrets do I hold inside?

We fear telling others a lot of things, such as judgments we have passed upon ourselves and are unwilling to release. Each person has to decide for themselves what they are willing to share and what they aren't. We can't judge another for this decision. It's important we honor and respect what they choose to do. We want to live our lives according to our own code of honor. What do we want for ourselves—that's what we should give to another? If we want truth, love, and commitment, then we need first to give this to ourselves and then to another. Once we can do this, we stand a better chance of possibly receiving it in return.

It's time to make our lives richer—that doesn't mean by making more money; it means by living your life from your heart, by being true to yourself, and by honoring the person you love.

CHAPTER 27

How We Relate
to Each Other

Relationships are wondrous things. They are agreements between two people to relate to each other in some way or other. How do we relate to others? How do they relate to us? While some people treat us well, others may not. What do we do when people treat us in a way that isn't comfortable? Do we speak up and tell them how we feel, or do we hide out, not saying a word? What do we allow others to do to us? What do we allow ourselves to do to those around us? Our goal is to look at the kind of relationships we want to have, then start working our way toward them. How do we do this? By working every day to improve the communications and ways of relating we have with each other.

Listen inside to what you want for yourself. Know that if it's something you want others to do for you, it's also something you should be willing to do for them. Begin to shape the relationships in your life so they are more conducive to the lifestyle you wish to live. No, you can't change other people, but you can change the way you choose to relate to them. This in itself can be enough to change the dynamics of a relationship. Try to do what you can to improve your present relationships. Know your every effort makes a difference. Treat the people in your life, yourself included, with the utmost respect. Your life might not be what you want it to be immediately, but in time you will have more and more of the respect you want from those around you if you are willing to first put it out there yourself. In some situations, you might not be able to create change through your behavior alone; leaving you to choose whether the relationship is of benefit for you to participate in any longer. You might find it necessary to end some relationships. This won't be easy, but it will be beneficial if it removes someone from your life who isn't respectful of who you are.

In looking at our own behavior and interaction in our relationships, we want to ask ourselves if we are contributing to what takes place. If we are, how can we change our own behavior? Maybe we can refuse to be pulled into certain types of conversations and interactions. How can we refuse? We can state our refusal verbally, or we can choose to change the subject when something that's of no benefit to anyone comes up. We can get pulled into gossiping about what other people should have done in their lives. Do we really have all the answers? This kind of communication benefits no one.

Gossip is a dangerous weapon, though we don't choose to see it as such. It undermines you as well. It's best to let go of your thoughts along this line. It will take some practice and some work on your part, but you will be better off by putting your energy in a more positive direction.

Open your heart. Allow people in who you might not normally allow. Just because these people aren't completely acceptable to you doesn't mean they don't have value and don't deserve to be treated with love and respect. What do we think we deserve? Do we deserve to be treated better than someone else? Why? What is it about us or our situation that elevates us above another? Whatever it is, it's not true. We all are of value. Yes, some of us may be more successful in outward appearances, but that doesn't make us of more value than someone else who isn't.

We can increase our ability to love and be loved by being more compassionate with those around us.

Our Patterns of Interacting with Others

Why do we want to be in a relationship? What do we hope to gain? Is it companionship you want, or do you simply miss not having a physical relationship? What do you want from the relationships in your life? If you don't have a special relationship with one person, maybe what you have instead is an opportunity to be true to yourself in the many various relationships you have with other people. Once you can be true to yourself—and love and honor yourself—you are ready for a more committed relationship with someone other than the friends that surround you. If you don't have friends surrounding you and you feel very much alone in the world, you might choose to look at how you treat yourself and those who you come into contact with on a daily basis. Are you loving? Are you kind? What do you choose to share with the strangers around you? Do you share everything with them or nothing at all? It's extremely useful to look at our patterns of relating to and interacting with others. We might want to change some of our ways of being in the world.

It's to our benefit to learn to be kind, compassionate, and loving. If we can do that for ourselves, we will have created a strong sense of self. If we can do that for the people around us, we will have more love and light to bring into the world. Our basic human drive is to be loved and to share more and more of ourselves with those around us. Don't be unkind to someone just because you don't know them or don't understand why they are the way they are. Decide kindness is all you want to put out into the world. When you find yourself saying something unkind about someone, change your message, change your thoughts. Try instead to find something kind and supportive to say, and if that's not possible, then leave the person alone.

Consider the consequences if we are held accountable for our thoughts and our actions in the world. Can you imagine what the world would be like if we could all read each other's minds? It's too overwhelming to even contemplate if you aren't used to monitoring your thoughts. What we can do not only for ourselves but for those we love is to learn to walk this earth from a place of peace and love from within ourselves. As we move closer to accomplishing this, we will have more to give and to share with those around us. It's time we do this. It's time we learn to 1) listen within and trust our inner voice, 2) respect other people and their choices, and also 3) love and respect ourselves as well, for until we do this, we will continually be asking someone else to give us what we need—and that won't always work out the way we want.

Love yourself, trust yourself. No, life won't always go the way you want it to, but if you are willing to stand beside yourself in total love and support, you will have achieved a great deal. You will have a lot of love and stability to share not only with yourself but with each person who enters your life.

Being More Effective in Relationships

Love may be present between the two of you, but unless you are willing to do the work involved, the commitment isn't solid. You can't have a commitment to the relationship unless you consciously decide to be in the relationship, to stay in the relationship, and to do the work it takes to do these things.

It takes a lot of work to have a healthy, strong, supportive relationship with another person. You can't keep sweeping things under the rug. You have to bring your issues out into the light. When two people communicate honestly with each other, it creates a bond between them that nothing can break. This bond will exist even when the other person is absent from your life.

Detach, trust, and let go when you are in a relationship. It may sound strange to hear the words detach in regard to being in a relationship. How do you detach from someone you love? You simply retain your ability to view the experience of relationship from a more balanced perspective. You retain your inner freedom. You view what occurs at the same time you participate. You become more conscious of the part you play in your own life and in the lives of others. This you can do by staying objective and watching everything that happens. When you can do this more, your relationships will stop being such huge dramas and become more stable. You will be more *effective* in communicating what you need and want, and thus be more effective in your relationships.

As we work to love, support, and value ourselves, we must also keep our hearts and minds open to each other. We will get from our relationship only what we are willing to give to it. A relationship depends on the ability of both people to give of themselves.

We have relationships in our lives that we don't think much about—perhaps it's a parent, a friend, a relative of some sort. What purpose do they serve? Do we take for granted the people who always seem to be there? They are in our lives for a reason. They bring things to us, and they need things from us. An exchange goes on whether we are aware of it or not, and it can have a positive effect on us or a negative one. Look at these people, at these relationships because they are all present to teach us something.

Though we seem independent of each other, there are so many ways we are connected to and interdependent upon each other.

It's important to love and depend on the people in our lives. Perhaps we have carried independence too far in the past. It's time to let go of some of our independent ways and become more a part of the lives of those who love and care for us. When we can do this, we will have a life that's interwoven with special people who love and support us as we love and support ourselves. Isn't this what you want for yourself, a life of love and support?

When we can see and value the beauty of each person, each relationship, our world will sparkle like never before.

CHAPTER 28
To Give and to Receive

When it comes to helping others and allowing others to help us, it's essential to move forward with compassion in our hearts. In our culture, we are taught how to reach out and help others, thus feeling good about the part we could play in making their lives a little better, their hearts a little lighter. What we have failed to learn in equal balance is to ask for, or be open to receiving, help ourselves. Somehow we have deemed it of value to give, but not to receive. What do we do when the hard times come?

Detach from all that's occurring in your life. Trust that somehow everything is going to work out. Take the time to stop and look at the lives of the people who surround you. What challenges do they face? It's time we notice others more because a great deal is happening in everyone's life. Try not to become so overwhelmed with your own life that you are unable to reach out a helping hand to those around you. When people come to you asking for help, help those who it's in your heart to help. You might have to turn some people away. You can't please everyone, so don't try. Do what you can, and then allow yourself to rest. With so much turmoil and chaos in the world today, we have to pay attention to what is happening and trust that somehow we will make it through it.

Detach, trust and let go over and over. When you can do this, you will be able to move through your life in a more fulfilling way. Detach from all that occurs. Trust you will have what you need. Let go of what is not most essential. Are you asking what this has to do with relationships? It has everything to do with you and how you interact with others. Observe the quality of your interactions with those around you and what they have to say. Watch how you choose to deal with every life situation. The more you can detach and trust that things will work out, the less stress you will feel. The less stress you feel, the less likely you will be to react to a situation in a way that could prove damaging to yourself and to others.

Detach, trust, and let go. Move on with your life. One day at a time, live your life as fully as you can. Some people will live their lives in a very quiet way; others will choose lives filled with a tremendous amount of activity. Whatever is present for you, trust it, detach from it and do the best you can. All you can do at this point is to love yourself as much as possible. Detach from thinking your life should be other than it is. Try to trust what occurs in your life is present to teach you something of value. Try to learn as much as you possibly can from your present life situation. Don't try to change too much about your life; the changes will come on their own. If we try to force changes into being, we can damage ourselves and our lives even more.

These are challenging times for everyone. Some people would love to live their lives in a way that's more beneficial to them and to those around them. This isn't always possible. For some reason, there are situations in life we are meant to experience. We cannot escape them. It's only when we surrender to the situation that we will learn all that is possible for us to learn. It's important to pay attention to our lives—and to live our lives as fully as we possibly can. If we can detach, trust, and let go, over and over and over again, *we can remain free of our circumstances.*

To take the best care of yourself under these conditions, 1) take one step at a time, 2) listen within, and 3) acknowledge what your inner guidance tells you. If there is something you need and it's possible for you to give it to yourself; do it. If it doesn't seem important, then let it go. Detach, trust, and let go. This will help you make it through any adversity that arises.

It's time we all begin to help each other more. How do you do this—one step at a time. Don't volunteer to do anything that's not in your heart to do, but if there is something that needs to be done and you want to be of assistance, then offer your help. It will be hard to turn people down at times, but this is important if you are trying to follow your inner guidance and be true to yourself. Initially, this could seem selfish to you, to turn someone down in their hour of need just because you don't feel like doing it. Watch what occurs when you try to force yourself to do something you really don't want to do. The resentment can run deep. In the long run, you will most likely find that, in truth you didn't so much help as you did injure yourself and your relationship with the person involved. Do what you can, and then let the rest go. Listen within and be willing to be true to yourself.

It's time we all begin to work together more. It's essential to start healing our relationships with each other. Many of you will find yourselves placed in difficult situations in order to make you reach out to someone you might not otherwise ask for help. When you reach out, you will find yourself in a vulnerable state. Being vulnerable is difficult for a lot of people—and we might try to hide our vulnerability. We want to seem to be in control of our lives even if we aren't. We want others to view us as being successful in our own right. It's difficult when we find we are unable to truly care for ourselves or others in our life unless we receive help from someone else. Why are we placed in these situations? What is present for us to learn? Could humility be the lesson? *Letting others help us as we would help them could be the plan.* Who knows what it is. All we can do is surrender to it, do what needs to be done, and know we are worth loving regardless of what does or doesn't happen in our lives. This is a challenging lesson to learn. It takes great perseverance and much humility. Be prepared to learn from this and to move on to whatever is next for you.

Perhaps you don't like the lessons that are present for you. What can you do about it? You can fight it, you can resist, but will that really change anything? Will that help you in any way, or will it only add further harm to a situation that is already almost too difficult to bear? Decide for yourself what you think should happen. What will be the best thing for you and for those you love? It's hoped you will stay present in this life to learn from these experiences. Often people will feel that too much is being asked of them. They will choose destructive methods in order to alleviate the pain they feel. Being destructive is no answer. There is no solution to be found in trying to escape from your life in this manner. It will only make things even more intense and that much more difficult.

Decide to take the best care of yourself regardless of what happens in your life. You are not your life. Your life has a life of its own. You don't create everything present in your life from this experience alone. A lot of factors figure into your present life. Tell yourself that no matter what you are experiencing, it's just passing through. In a matter of time, it will all change into something else. Possibly you are afraid of what this something else might be? All you can do for yourself is trust that somehow you will have the strength, honor, and integrity to deal with it. You will do it one step at a time. Don't look ahead into the future. Most people won't have a future they can identify anyway. All you can do is detach, trust, love, and let go, over and over again.

Take good care of yourself. Love yourself; love those around you. Try to be as patient as you can with yourself and with others. This will make a big difference in your life as well as in theirs. We are living in a time of great change and a time of chaos and turmoil. Do what you can to bring peace and contentment to your life.

Be willing to help when possible; be open to receiving help when needed. Live only in the present moment. Find peace there, and you will have found a great source of strength and wisdom.

Chapter 29

Facing the Truth of the Situation

Relationships are problems and we have yet to discover the solutions. How can they be problems? Because they are beyond our ability to know and to understand. We can't possibly know and understand the motives of another person. They do things and say things that are foreign to us at times. We want to understand, and we might even find a way to rationalize what is happening, but deep down we know we don't have a clue to what is really transpiring.

Allow the other person to come to you with an explanation for their actions. They could decide to tell you the absolute truth, or they might decide to tell you what they think you will want to hear. How will you know the difference? You will know deep within yourself. You might not be willing to admit you know, but you will. You may decide what you want to live with is the lie that comes from their lips. The truth might be too much for you to bear.

The kind of a relationship you have when two people can't share the truth with each other—is one built on deception. It's one person deceiving the other because they are unable to face the truth of the situation. Then you have the main character deceiving themselves because they don't really want to hear the truth. What can you do to change this situation? You can begin to face the truth as you know and understand it. You can say to the person you are involved with that you feel there's more to what is happening, that perhaps they have left something out. To do this, however, you have to be willing to risk the loss of trust within your relationship. *Trust is a very fragile, very important part of all relationships.* As long as we convince ourselves that we can trust the person we are in a relationship with, we seem to have our most basic need covered. What occurs, however, when we discover the person we care so deeply for has been telling us something other than the truth? We begin to also doubt all else they have been telling us. We doubt them, the value of our relationship, and the value of our part in their life. All at once our relationship is filled to overflowing with the doubts we have about the other person's dependability and honesty.

What happens to us when we find we no longer trust the person with whom we want to share our life? We begin a process of separation. We might not physically separate, but part of us inside will pull back to protect the vulnerable parts of ourselves. It's essential to know we can trust the person we love. What happens when this trust is injured? What will we choose to do then? It will be different for each person. Some people will be accepting of the lies they are told because they don't want, or expect, much more from the person with whom they are involved. Why are their expectations so low? Conceivably because they have yet to have a relationship of greater integrity in their life. It takes inner strength to withstand the truth of what another person might say to us. Some people don't want to know what the real truth is because it will jeopardize the stability of their life. Change is difficult for many people. They might settle for less than what they deserve because they fear having to make any changes in their life.

Ask yourself:

- What amount of truth can I stand to hear?
- How do I avoid the truth?
- How do I conspire with another to keep my life stable and away from the verge of breaking up?
- How demanding am I of the answers another gives me as to the reasons for the behavior I fail to understand? Realize that behavior is a surface action you can see, but the *motivation* for that behavior lies deeply buried within the person with whom you are interacting.
- Do I really want to understand why they do the things they do?
- Do I really want to know why they fail to be present in love when that's all I want from them?

These are important questions. Until you are willing and able to hear the truth, it's unlikely you will receive it.

Why do we choose to hide from our true feelings and our reactions to people and things? To not hide means confronting some inner demons that may not be acceptable to us. By acceptable, we might not be able to see or accept what we do that could injure or harm another person. When we can't accept ourselves or our behavior, we find an excuse that justifies our actions. However, what do we do when the person we are in a relationship with calls us on this behavior? Do we tell them the real reason for our behavior, or do we tell them what we want them to hear? It all depends on your ability to love and to accept yourself. At times people are greatly threatened by any insight their partner has of them. It means they aren't worth loving. Where do we get this idea? Is it the truth? The truth is that we are all worth loving, but sometimes we exhibit behaviors that need to be confronted and released. How do we release a behavior if we are unwilling to see it or if we can't stand to have another person tell us about it because we perceive it to mean we have no value? We have value—and it's important to believe and trust that above all else. At times others might not treat us like this is the case, but what's essential is that we treat ourselves with the love and respect we deserve. Doing so doesn't excuse our behavior, but it gives us the strength to face it and to possibly make some changes within our way of being in the world.

What a gift you give to yourself when you become willing to learn from any and all of life's situations. It's only when you are open to learning that you will truly begin to grow more whole within yourself. We become separated from ourselves when we can accept so little of ourselves and our behaviors. It takes courage to stop explaining away our behavior and face the truth. Yes, truth changes a lot depending upon how you choose to perceive it, but to perceive it at all means you face it in some capacity. With love for ourselves, our work is to face the truth of every situation in which we find ourselves. It's only when we can face the truth that we will have a true and honest relationship with ourselves and with others.

Excellent relationship questions:

- What do you want for yourself?
- What do you want for the person who shares your life?
- Is it too late in your relationship to tell the truth?
- Do you feel your relationship is beyond saving?
- If you do, what are you willing and able to do about it?

- Don't you want more for yourself?

What are you willing to do to get it? Do you realize it all starts with you? It's not the other person's fault for how your life is; it's up to you. Be willing to take responsibility for the choices you have made in life so far. This doesn't mean you have to continue on in the way you always have, but it does mean you will accomplish nothing by blaming another person for what you helped create.

It's time to look at your life, as well as your relationships. How much of your life is based on truth? How much of your life is a deception of one sort or another? What is the quality of the relationship you want to have with yourself and with another person? You decide this by each answer you give when you are asked to explain your behavior away. Next time dare to be honest. Dare to be yourself. Stop trying to protect yourself by telling stories that might not be true. Try to use these occasions as opportunities to learn and to grow. Confront the darkness that lies within you. Be willing to bring parts of yourself out into the light. When you are willing to do this, they will lose their power over you. They will no longer be a painful, difficult part of you. They will have been exposed to the light. And if you are willing to do the work necessary, you can transform these dark areas into areas of love and of light. Please be willing to do this work for yourself. Once you are willing to do it, you will learn and grow so much from your sharing. You will come to love and accept yourself as a human being. When you can do this for yourself, you can do this for others as well. You will stop being so critical of yourself. You will stop demanding so much from those around you. This is important work. Take it one step at a time, one step in love, one step in patience and one step in kindness. Learn to love and accept yourself. In turn you will also love and accept others.

What is more important than loving and accepting ourselves? If we can't love and accept ourselves, how do we expect to bring more love into the world? If we don't bring more love into the world, what do we expect to have for ourselves? Do we always expect the love we want to come from a place external to us? How can it exist for us in another person when we don't feel it for ourselves? What happens when the person you are in a relationship with begins to find flaws in you? When they begin to point out things about you they don't like or find difficult to live with, do you accuse them of not loving you enough, or do you listen patiently and decide for yourself if what they are telling you is really the truth and possibly will require some work and some change on your part? How do we open ourselves to becoming a part of the process of change? How can we take criticism without injuring or damaging ourselves? Because we are worth loving doesn't mean we are a perfect human being without any flaws or shortcomings. If we can understand that there are behaviors we all hold within ourselves that would benefit us to change, maybe we will have a chance at accepting ourselves even when we feel extremely open and vulnerable to another's words or requests.

The more open and vulnerable we can be, the more honest our relationships will be also. It's important to love and support ourselves during these times of openness and vulnerability. It's not necessary to rush to our own defense to prove we are worth loving. If we work on loving ourselves, we will understand this truth along with the acceptance that yes, there may be some behaviors that would be beneficial to change. We don't have to punish ourselves for not being right about everything. Where do we get some of these patterns? Yes, our childhood is a source; however we might never come to understand the other sources.

It's important we come to love and trust ourselves. Once we can do this, we can afford to be honest in our communications with another because we will know that regardless of what occurs, we are loved.

CHAPTER 30

Surrendering Tendencies That Could Injure Others

We can prepare ourselves for the days ahead by listening within more and paying attention to everything that occurs around us. When we can do this, we will be able to move through our life feeling the love that's in our heart. We will be better able to love ourselves and others. This awareness is important because it will give us the strength and courage to endure the challenges that come our way. It's only when we can love from our heart that we will be able to give not only to ourselves, but also to others. It's this giving, this sharing, that will make all the difference in our lives.

What do we have to share with each other? We have a great deal, but at times, you may feel you have nothing of value to give to someone else. That isn't true. You have so much to share. Your presence alone is of great value. Why do you fail to realize this? What prevents you from being aware of the inner beauty that you are? Perhaps you simply don't believe you are special in any way.

You are very, very special, but so then is everyone else. At times, you have to look deeply to find out what is precious about another person, but keep looking because it's there. That quality of special-ness is within each of us and is what we have to share with each other. We all come together with different gifts and personalities. We can prepare ourselves to share the gift of who we are, but we also need to be willing to surrender some of the tendencies we have that could be injuring other people.

How can our tendencies injure other people? If you have the tendency to always arrive late, it could injure your ability to be with others because they would simply choose to give up on your being present when you say you will. That injures not only you, but your relationships with them as well. It's helpful to look at our relation-ships and try to see what qualities we have that might not be of benefit to us. We do and say many things we might want to change. The first step is being aware of what you do or say that injures another, or causes distress in those with whom you are trying to have a healthy relationship. It could be you are unable to see these qualities until they are pointed out to you by another—maybe you have no desire to see what you are being told about yourself. It's time to listen to what others have to say to you. *This is your oppor-tunity to learn.* Why should you want to learn? So you can improve your relationship with yourself and with those around you. Why should this matter? Because the quality of your life depends upon what you have to share and what others are willing to share with you. Do you want the quality of your life to improve, or are you satisfied to stay where you are right now?

It's time we all pay attention to how we interact with the peo-ple in our lives. Our behavior is important. It's important as to how we choose to treat ourselves. Listen to what others have to say. Perhaps there are a few adjustments you could make in your behavior so you will be more compatible in your relationships.

Why would you feel threatened if you are being asked to make these changes? Could it be because you choose to perceive it as someone telling you that you aren't perfect the way you are? Is that what you expect from yourself, perfection? Take time to reevaluate yourself and your expectations of self. Cut yourself some slack because none of us are perfect. The words of another can help us be aware of behaviors we have that cause difficulties in our relationships. Our work is to be open to learning and to be willing to let go of behaviors that only injure us as well as our relationships.

We can do this work if we can:

- Listen to what another has to say.
- Love ourselves in spite of anything that is said to us. We aren't suddenly unworthy of someone else's love just because they don't approve of everything we do or say.
- Be reasonable with each other.
- Learn to communicate our thoughts, feelings, and needs.
- Tell each other what is bothering us.
- Explore our difficulties with each other. It's not necessary to throw away every relationship we have because we hit a bumpy road.

There is so much to learn—and share with each other. Let's do it now, and do it together. Let's do it with love and compassion for each other and especially for ourselves. Detach, trust and let go, over and over again. We can make it through this process of knowing each other, this process of learning to know even ourselves much better. Begin this work today. Trust that you will be alright regardless of what another person chooses to say or do. You will be alright if only you choose to believe it and to take the steps necessary to take good care of yourself throughout this process of love and change.

It adds to our stability to trust that we can make changes within ourselves. When we do make changes, we are doing it for the best reason of all: because we love and care for ourselves. It's only when we do it for ourselves and do it from our heart that the changes will truly take and benefit us and everyone we love. It's time to detach more from our lives, to trust everything that occurs, and to be willing to let go and listen to the words others have to say. This doesn't always mean it's us who need to change. Sometimes the other person needs to change how they are choosing to perceive a particular situation. Whatever occurs, the only thing you can do is to be present in love for yourself, trust what you know inside, and be willing to share your thoughts.

Try to make your life more of a learning experience. Begin to look at your relationships in a different way. Begin to perceive them as opportunities to learn with and from another person. You don't have to know more than they do to be of value. That isn't the issue. The issue is: do you love yourself, and are you able to learn and grow? Ask yourself these questions. If you answer no, you might want to explore the reasons why you choose to withhold the love you deserve from yourself, or why you fear making any changes?

It's important to be present in love for ourselves. Listen within and honor what you think and feel. Do be careful not to take the pain you feel out on another. The pain you feel inside is your pain. It could be the pain of abandonment, the pain of hate, fear or some other emotion. Feel this pain, explore it, embrace it, and then choose to let it go. If at all possible, don't take it out on another person. It's not another person who gives you this pain. Perhaps they set up a situation that enables you to get in touch with the pain you feel, but they aren't responsible for the pain. Dealing with surfacing pain is a complex issue to understand, but in time, if you choose to use this as an opportunity to explore the pain that presents itself, you will come to understand that *you are the one who holds this pain within you.* Your relationship with another can bring this pain to the surface for you to experience and feel, but it's not always their fault you feel this pain. Occasionally, the situation makes it appear that it's someone else's fault—and we all do need to be held responsible for our behavior, for the part we play in each other's life, but next time the pain arises, try to understand where it's really coming from within you. Talk about it, let it out. Begin to explore these issues of pain and release. It's important we do this work, for it will lighten our spirits and allow us to love each other more fully.

The healing process requires us to be willing to experience, explore, and release our pain—and to share our thoughts and feelings with each other. It's necessary to allow ourselves to be vulnerable not only with ourselves, but also with others. We can do this *work of learning to love and accept ourselves.* When we do this work, we share with others the process of change that will occur within us, for we can't uncover these truths and not reveal ourselves, our lives, and our experiences.

As we come to love ourselves and to trust what we know inside is our truth, it's imperative we share our love and our truth. Come to know and love yourself. Believe that there is someone out there who will eventually benefit from being your friend, from being your lover, and from being in your life. It may take time, and you might have to go through a lot of relationships that seem only to be major life disappointments, but don't settle for less than you know in your heart you deserve. You deserve the best, so prepare yourself to give it as well. Meanwhile, fill your life with things of value to you; they don't always have to be worldly possessions. They can be things of value that bring honor to you and to your life.

Do the best you can to participate in your life in a way that's most beneficial to you and to those with whom you share your days. Bring a little more love and a little more light into each and every day. You can do it, and you will do it in a way that is special and unique to you.

CHAPTER 31

Take the Time to Nourish Relationships

W e want to teach ourselves to be kind and loving to ourselves under any and all conditions. Once we can do this for ourselves, we can begin to do it for others. Being kind and loving is critical at this time in our life history. Pressures in our lives greatly stress our relationships. The more we can step forth into the world from a place of love within ourselves, we will be better able to cope with everything that occurs.

It's time we begin to talk to and listen to each other. How do we expect to do this when we are all so busy that we don't have the time to do it? It's vital we slow down the movement in our lives. We need to *choose our priorities* very carefully. For everything we choose to include in our daily life—something is left out.

Ask yourself:

- What am I choosing to include?
- What's most important to me?

- What am I choosing to release?
- Is it my children or my partner I am releasing?

Be careful in the decisions you make, for it's easy to get so busy with work, with life, and with living that you don't take the time for the most important relationships in your life.

What happens when you don't take the time to nourish important relationships? You lose them. People drift away. They no longer feel the pull to be with you because you aren't there to be with them. This creates a lot of difficulty in your life because you are still attached to these people you love, so their decision not to be in your life could affect you very deeply. Why do you take for granted that they will stay? Do you take for granted they will stay, or are you trying to push them out and away? What reason would you have for doing that? Maybe it's too much to do all you do and to still maintain personal relationships that require time, energy, and commitment on your part. Look at what you pull toward you and look at what you push away. Be honest with yourself about why you do what you do.

It's time to look at your life and make some conscious choices. What do you want in your life? Who do you want in your life? Only the most important things and people will survive the changes that lie ahead. This means with all that goes on in your life, it will be difficult to hold on to anything that doesn't really matter. You won't have the energy to do so as all your energy will be tied up in the things you choose to fill your days. It will require all your time, energy, and focus for the people and the things that are important to you. Limit what you do and limit the people with whom you choose to spend your time. Don't try to spread yourself so thin that you have no time and energy left for yourself at the end of the day. This might not always be possible, but it's a good thing to keep in mind. You want to somehow make time and space in your life also for yourself. Do this by considering yourself of special value. Realize the needs you have, and commit yourself to meeting some of them.

We all have needs: 1) For some people it's to be alone, to have time to contemplate their life and what's occurring in it. 2) For some people it's to have a lot of physical activity. 3) For some people it's to place themselves in positions where they are helping other people. What are your needs? Realize what they are and commit yourself to meeting them. You don't have to be rigid in the schedule you keep for yourself, but don't put yourself off too much or for too long. In order to continue operating in life in a healthy manner, you want to somehow nourish yourself in the meantime. Identify your needs and find the necessary ways of making your life beneficial to yourself. When you can do this, you will be recharging yourself and bringing extra energy that's needed into your body system.

Why is it essential to take such good care of ourselves? Because *the basis for any good relationship with another is a good relationship with yourself.* Until you can form a bond of love and commitment with yourself, you will be unable to do so with another. To commit to loving another might seem easy because of the feelings you have inside, but what happens when these feelings change? You can't control your feelings? What do you do when your feelings for another change? When you have invested all you are in another person and then your feelings for them change, you will find yourself in a situation where you feel as if you have lost everything, yourself included. How do you prevent this from happening? The only thing you can do is love yourself every inch of the way. If you have a base of love for yourself, it will be easy to share that love with another. If or when the time comes that you find your feelings have changed for the other person in your life, it will be easier to support yourself in love and compassion during any changes you find necessary to make.

Why do we need to make so many changes in our lives? This is a time of great change on our planet. Things seem to be moving at a much faster rate. So much more information is available to all of us. The pressures and the stress we live under truly seem to be increasing. It's definitely a challenge to keep ourselves and our relationships in a state of good health. In order to do the best job we can, we want to be awake and aware of what's going on in our life and in the lives of those around us. If we close ourselves off from the people we love, it won't be long before we become strangers to each other. We want to be careful to keep our lines of communication open and clear by continually recommitting to our relationships.

What does it mean to *commit* yourself? It means to make something or someone a priority in your life. In order to do this, you want to stop putting things or people on hold. You can't keep denying the people in your life the things they need from you. If you do, it won't be long before they are no longer willing to be there for you. How can you expect others to commit themselves to a relationship with you if you aren't willing to do the same for them? To commit doesn't just mean you show up at the same house at the end of the night. It means you commit to putting time and energy into something or someone. You can't do this unless you take the time necessary to do so. You can't commit to someone or something and then not follow through on your words with the necessary action.

People frequently make verbal commitments to each other but then never do anything to reinforce what they have said. It isn't enough to just say you commit yourself to another; you have to prove it. You are called upon to show through your behavior that you really care, which doesn't mean you continually deny yourself and the person you care for the time to be together. Time has become an element in overwhelming demand these days. In order to stay together, you must be willing to spend time together. How else do you expect a relationship to survive? Because you loved each other once doesn't guarantee the love you felt will stay alive and grow; repeatedly, people take this for granted. Love isn't something you can take for granted; it's there or it's not. If it's there, be sure to nourish it. How many times do you find yourself telling a loved one, "Not now, I am too busy, soon, soon I will take the time?" "Soon" may not be soon enough if you continue to place other things or people as priorities in your life. You maybe don't even consider these other things as priorities; they could just be things you think you have to do or get done. When all the getting done is completed, which it rarely ever is, who is there waiting for you—possibly no one. Is that what you want? What can you do to prevent this from happening?

To love and nourish our relationships with ourselves and with others it's of value to:

- Take essential alone time, and also time to be with those we cherish. When we are unable to do this, we risk losing a great deal. We can't expect people to be there for us when we are rarely there for them. This creates a void in our relationships. Relationships require an investment of energy to keep them alive. No matter how much you love someone, if you are unwilling or unable to continue to put energy into the relationship, you will, in time, lose the person you care for because they will grow tired of waiting for you to come to your senses.

- Value relationships. The people who surround us are of value. It's imperative we see this, feel this, and take care to nourish these relationships. Do you want someone to love you completely—and to commit their life to being with you? How do you expect to receive this type of commitment if you are unable to love and nourish the relationships in your life? Yes, we expect a lot from the people in our lives, and we don't realize the commitment we must make as our part of the deal.

- Be willing to make this type of a commitment. Be willing to take the time necessary to love and nourish your relationships. It's the only way you will have any relationships of strength and value. Commit yourself to loving the people in your life. Tell them and show them, and you will be amazed at the flow of love and of life that's there for you to enjoy.

Choosing between Something and Someone You Love

It's difficult to give up the things in life that are important to you. Why should you, you ask? Because there will come a time when you are asked to choose between something and someone you love. This will be a difficult choice to make. Someone will lose something along the way. What do you stand to lose? It could be the person you love. It might be a child with whom you truly want to spend more time. What are you having to give up? What are you asking of yourself? Why are you having to do this? These are key questions because this is a pivotal time in your life.

What are you willing to give up, to release in order to have some of the things you want in life? At times we don't even realize we are making this decision, we ease into it because we start to work and don't notice what we are losing as time passes. Why do we work? To support ourselves, or is it much, much more? For some people, the work they do only gets them from paycheck to paycheck. They can't conceive there's any other choice to what they do. Other people make more than enough money, but they are so obsessed with what they do, they are unable to stop and let it go at any one point.

What do you do with your time? Why do you choose what you choose? Respect your need to make a living, but also be willing to look at the reasons you have for feeling compelled to earn more money than what buys you a comfortable life. It seems there is always something to want. What can you do without? Why should you have to do without? A time may come in your relationship with another when you are asked to choose between them and the work you do. You might not think you have a choice, but you do. Many people sacrifice so much out of a fear of not having their needs met. What if we could all relax a little more, trust we will have what we need, and begin to place our priorities in a way that will be more beneficial to us all? How do we do this? It's done by trusting your life more. It might seem extremely challenging at times, but somehow it all works out. If only we can relax a little more and trust our lives to take the course it needs to take. That amount of trust does require a considerable amount of letting go. Let go of worrying about everything, every detail of your life, and trust yourself, knowing you are of value regardless of what occurs. Many changes will come to us all; the more grace with which we greet them will make a tremendous difference for us and for those we love. When asked to make changes, be careful what you choose for yourself. Make your choices out of love, not out of fear. Don't be afraid you won't have what you need. Begin to practice telling yourself, "I will always have my basic needs met. I will trust this." Difficult times may be ahead, but if you can trust this basic premise, you will have more faith than most. It's beneficial to start doing this work of trusting. It will positively affect your life and the lives of those around you. Begin to do this. Do it for yourself. Do it for your children. Do it for all the people you love. Trust that somehow you will have your needs met, and then be careful to watch to see how it will occur.

Begin to pay attention to the choices you make in your life.

- Where are you right now?
- Where do you someday hope to be? Be careful what you choose for yourself. Is there life in your choices, or are you dooming yourself to living a life that's totally unfulfilling for you?
- What price are you willing to pay for all the material goods you so think you need to have?
- Is the price too great?
- How do you treat the people in your life?
- Do you want to spend more time with them?

It's important we take responsibility for the choices we make and realize the gravity of these choices. How will we be able to tell that what we choose is really for the best? If you feel peace, joy, and contentment after you've made your choice, that will be a good indication the choice you've made has been a good one for you. Be patient with yourself; be as kind as you can be. Know the choice you make is a difficult one, but make the one that will bring you toward the life you want to live. You might not understand how you will be able to make it in the world if you choose what in your heart you so want to choose, but if you can trust a little more than you do now, you will have your answer soon enough. Trust yourself, trust your life, and be willing to make some choices that take a significant amount of courage. You will still have what you need; it will just come to you in a way that's different from what you have previously experienced.

If we can start to take more time for each other and stop all the noise and distractions that prevent us from doing so, we can strengthen our relationships. We have truly lost the ability to take time for each other. It seems we have so little time these days; how can we stop just to talk to someone else? After all, we have so much we have to get done.

What can be more important than talking with, or listening to, someone who may need our help or guidance? What has more value? It's time to look at the choices we are making in our everyday life. It's so easy to slip into the mode of getting things done, then collapsing on the couch. If possible, let go of a few more things and take the time to communicate with each other. All our relationships suffer when we fail to talk with each other. It's our communication; our caring for each other that holds us all together. What takes place when the communication stops and it seems we have no time to spend together? How can you help but drift apart?

Make some conscious choices about what you want in your life. Do you want your present job, or do you want time with your spouse/partner and family? Why do you have to choose? You have to choose only if your job is asking so much of you that you stand to lose the people who are most important to you. Begin to look at this. Begin to draw your boundaries so you can protect and nourish the relationships with those you love the most. At times, we think if we sacrifice ourselves by giving all our time and energy to our jobs that our family or loved ones should understand. They will understand for a while, but then when, time after time, you fail to be present when they need you, they will begin to move away from you. It will only be a matter of time before they build their lives without you in it. Is that what you want? Why can't you seem to do something about it? What stops you? Are you too tied up in what you need from your work? Perhaps your identity is too tied up with all the acknowledgments you get at work. Are you too tired to deal with it all? Whether you are tired or not, your life will continue on without you if you are unwilling or unable to participate. We can be a part of each other's lives in many, many ways. You don't always have to be there in person to be an active part of someone's life, but if you want to be, take notice of the time and attention you can give to another— this makes a big difference.

Observe your life and the direction it takes. Does it leave your loved ones behind? If it does, what will you choose to do about it? Are you strong enough in yourself to do something to change what occurs? This could ask a lot from you. You might be unable to meet the demands of life that you usually greet with ease. Often when we make changes in our lives, it challenges us to our very core. It's helpful if we can remember why we have chosen the course we have. What do we have to gain? What do we have to lose if we continue on in the way we have been for so long? This can be a difficult life transition for some people; for others it may be exactly what they needed in order to survive. Judge for yourself what your most important priorities are, and then be willing to stand up for yourself. When you can do this, you will experience an inner strength you had no idea you possessed.

Trust yourself, trust your life. It will take you where you need to go. Make the choices you deem best to make. Trust everything that occurs as a result of those choices. Above all else…listen within and be cautious of taking the easy way out; it may not work for your benefit.

At times, it's necessary to take risks to have what is most important to us in life. Be willing to risk what you have to risk. Be willing to love and support yourself. Trust everything that occurs. Step by step you will make your way through it all and come out of it with a life more to your liking.

SECTION 7
GAINING STABILITY AND HAPPINESS WITHIN YOURSELF AND YOUR RELATIONSHIPS

CHAPTER 32
Trust the Love We Have for Ourselves

Relationships are fragile things. To help us understand how to deal with them, it's important to:
Be ourselves.

- Trust the love we have for ourselves.
- Share this love with another.
- Let go of a lot of the ways we think our life should be.
- Trust ourselves and the choices we make.
- Put one foot forward at a time.
- Trust we will have what we need in life.
- Stop living our lives out of fear.
- Trust and love ourselves more and more.

When we can do this we will have the life and the love we want for ourselves.

Detach from all that occurs in your life. Be determined to trust everything that happens. Trust what occurs and love yourself in spite of it. That's the only way you will make it through your life with an abundance of love surrounding you. If you can put the love there for yourself first, others will join you and add to the load. It's necessary to love and respect yourself first. Trust you are worth loving and you are worth another person wanting to be a part of your life. Having built this stronger level of trust, you will have the foundation for a life full of love and full of relationships of great value.

You can have a life full of love. You can have a life where you commit yourself to bringing as much love as possible into the world. What better thing is there to do in life? Perhaps love isn't that important to you. If that's the case, why is this true? What are you afraid of? Why do you hold back from loving yourself and those around you? What has happened to you that you don't feel yourself deserving of the love you try to give to others? Have you been hurt? How do you hope to heal those wounds if you don't allow yourself the love you know deep inside you want?

Know you can have a life full of love. Start today by doing something special for yourself. Give yourself a treat. Do it today, do it tomorrow, and do it each day after. You deserve to have a good life.

You will have love in your life. To have it you must be it.

CHAPTER 33

Trust What Happens in Your Life

Trust yourself. What does this mean? It means to trust everything that happens in your life. There are no accidents. Everything is in your life to teach you something. You may not be able to understand why it's there, but that doesn't really matter. What matters is that you understand it's there for your benefit. It's hard to trust this knowledge, but it's true. Embrace this concept and learn how to move through your life from a more centered place of being.

How can one be centered when one is surrounded by chaos? One can be centered when one learns to trust everything that occurs. When you have this trust within, nothing can take it away from you. Again there's much you won't understand, but when that happens, just tell yourself, "Though I don't understand, it's important I trust everything that occurs." This doesn't mean you are a victim of life.

Within chaos there are choices to be made.

- Make the best possible choices you can for yourself.
- Try not to blame another for what you experience.
- Take charge of your life in as far as how you choose to perceive what is happening.
- Perceive your present situation so it's beneficial to you.
- Perceive your present situation so you can learn the most from it?

This is what life is about, and what learning to trust and to love yourself is about. Having achieved this stance, you will be free of all the things that pull you away from your center of balance. You will stop making a drama out of your life. You will live your life in a much more balanced and peaceful manner. Choose what you want for yourself. Remember that how you choose to *perceive* your present situation determines how you move forth in life.

Trust your life. The things that happen in your life happen to teach you something. Be ready and open to learning and making some changes. Let go of your fear of change. Begin to think of life as more of an adventure instead of a constant struggle to achieve various goals.

When you trust what occurs, most if not all of your resistance will fall away. You will begin to trust yourself and your life process more and more. You will come to realize it's important you do this for others as well. You will be better equipped to honor the life process of others, and what they think and want for themselves. In order to honor everyone's life process, it's necessary to 1) stop *forcing* things in our lives, 2) *trust* we will have what we most need, 3) be prepared to *take responsibility* for our actions toward others, and 4) learn to *detach* from our lives and move forth from a more centered place of being.

Make the best choices you can. Regardless of what you do, occasionally, your life will take a course you don't want to experience. When this happens, be prepared to *surrender* to what is present. To resist will only bring you more pain than you already have. It can be difficult to surrender to certain life experiences. Look at the choices available for you to make. Perhaps there seems little to no choice at all. What are you going to do then? Are you going to surrender to the situation and make the best of it, learn from it and live within it, or are you going to fight until you can't fight anymore? Each person will make their own choice, but really look at what you are choosing to do to yourself and to others when you resist what's happening. In certain circumstances, the only choice might be how you are going to perceive the situation and how you are going to deal with it. There may be times when we so want to change our life, but it doesn't seem within our power to do so no matter how hard we try. When this occurs, are we going to surrender and make the best of it, or are we going to resist it and become destructive not only to ourselves but also to those we love? We make these choices every day. It serves us to become more conscious of the choices we are making.

Choose what you want for yourself. Know what you choose affects others in your life. What do you want to share with those around you? What do you want to tell them? Do you want to tell them that at times life can be very difficult, but what's really important is to love yourself and persevere? You need to teach yourself how to do this so you can have the best attitude possible. Once you can show this level of love, you will possess a solid core of *inner strength*. This inner strength will see you through the days ahead. It's this inner strength that will allow you to love yourself and to love those around you in spite of what's going on in your life. It's essential to get in touch with this inner strength and use it to our greatest benefit. Decide how best to use it. Would you use it to force your life to be different from what it is, or are you going to surrender to what is present and make the best life you can until something presents itself that enables a change to come about in a more effortless, productive manner? How you use your inner strength is your choice.

This work of trusting and loving yourself is essential to your own well-being. It will also affect everyone who comes into your life or is in your presence. Be kind and gentle with yourself. You don't control all aspects of your life. Yes, there will be rough spots. Decide to weather those rough spots with as much grace and as much love as possible.

It is important to stand back and look at the larger picture. We are here to learn. At times we get trapped into believing we are here just so we can have all the things we want in our life. That is part of life, but the lessons are also a part. Frequently we are totally unprepared to learn, and we resent the fact that life doesn't seem to be going how we think it should. When this happens we want to stop and ask ourselves, "Is there possibly something I have to learn from all of this?" If we can take time to be alone, we will be able to get in touch with our inner self. We can then focus more on the good things in our life. We will also realize the lessons that are there for us to learn. When we can do this, our resistance will be minimal. We will be able to survive within a situation with the minimal amount of stress. We will more fully be able to love ourselves and those around us. Is this not of tremendous value? To learn to love and trust yourself and your life regardless of what occurs is a great lesson. It's a very difficult one indeed, but it has so much value.

It's time we all come together in love and support not only for each other but also for ourselves. We need the love and support we can give ourselves. We gain stability if we can trust we will have what is most essential in life. This doesn't mean life will always be easy. We always have something to learn, and it isn't until we are able to process it all that we can come to understand the value a certain situation may hold.

Trust yourself and trust your life. Take good care of yourself so you can lead a life that's full in all ways. Full of love, full of caring, and full of sharing.

CHAPTER 34
Live in the
Present Moment

B e ready to look at your relationship. Be ready to look at yourself and your actions and behaviors. Be willing to speak up when someone does something that doesn't feel good to you. Ask them why they find it necessary to behave in that manner. Tell them what you are feeling as a result of their *present* behavior. If at all possible, leave the past in the past. Don't continually bring up all the painful experiences from past times. Too frequently, people make it a habit to feel sorry for themselves by living in the past. The past is the past; it's over, let it go. Get on with living your life in the here and now. If you have an issue to raise, raise it right away, don't wait until its part of the past and you are caught up in all your wounds.

It's important to live our lives fully in this present moment, aware of what's happening around us and to us. Our goal is to get in touch with our feelings. It could be we feel something, but it isn't until much later we can figure out what's happening within us. Why can't we be more present and aware to what we feel at the time we feel it? We might get confused because we don't understand what's happening. How can we understand more easily? By paying attention, by being willing to speak up for your own wants and needs, and also by taking the time to be alone. When we take time alone, it can be easier to figure out what's happening. The time we spend alone is very beneficial, it allows us to separate more from the person we are involved with and get a point of view that's more clearly our own. To gain clarity is necessary to balance ourselves within the relationship.

A busy life might leave you thinking you don't have time to stop and figure things out. What do you do with your thoughts and your feelings then? You stuff them. You think because your body has continued on to other projects, the rest of you will follow. It could seem that way for a brief period of time, but a part of you is lost to the issues at hand. When you deny yourself the time and energy it takes to clear up what's happening within you and within your relationship, you are a divided person. It's impossible to truly be at peace with yourself and with your life. When we aren't at peace, it's hard to give anyone or anything our full, undivided attention.

If we can keep ourselves present-moment focused and clear up issues as soon as they arise, we will have so much more peace and cooperation in all our important relationships. This present moment is where we live our lives. We can't live the future though we often lose ourselves in thinking we can. We can also lose ourselves to the past. If we can remind ourselves to let go of the past, let go of the future and live in this present moment alone, we will have honed our focus to exactly where our life is being lived. This present moment truly is all there is.

Living in the Past

When we live in the past, we limit our lives and our relationships. The past has to do with experiences we have had, hopefully worked through, and released. When we haven't done the work to release these experiences, we drag them forward with us into our present moments. They become a controlling factor in our lives. They color all the experiences we have from then forward. If we have done the work to process these past experiences, we can move forward, having learned what we needed to learn, and therefore become a lighter, more loving human being.

Living in the Future

If we choose to stay solely focused on what we want our future to be, we can lose sight of where we are in this present moment. If this present moment really is where we live our lives and we are continually focused on what is to come rather than what is happening in this moment, our whole life can pass us by without us fully experiencing what we have lived.

Does Anyone Really Know What the Future Holds?

When we want to prepare ourselves for the days ahead, ask yourself:

- How do I do this? By paying attention to what is occurring presently and not living off in the future somewhere.
- Is there someone I really want to be with but choose not to because I don't see a future together?
- Does that mean at this time there aren't precious moments we can share with each other?
- Does there always have to be a future?
- Does anyone really know what the future holds for them?

Observe how you choose to live your life. Are your choices made in the future, or are they made right here, based on what you know and feel in the present? It's of value to stop looking ahead and be more aware of the moment you are in. What are you afraid of? Are you afraid of making a mistake? Are you afraid of loving someone who may not be the *perfect* person for you? What happens if you love someone, yet they don't fulfill all your requirements for a partner in life? Does that make the relationship of any less value? Some would say yes, some would say no. It depends on what you want and expect out of the relationship.

Possibly you have a person in your life who is very special to you, but you hold them at arm's length because you are sure you'll meet a more perfect person. You don't want to hurt and disappoint this person so you hold back. What happens when you hold back? It could be they hold back as well. What does it feel like to hold back from someone you care a great deal about? What does it feel like to have someone hold back from you? Think about what you really want in your life. Do you want to love, or do you want to hold off for the perfect person? Do you really believe there is a perfect person, or even a person who is more suitable? If you do believe there is, you will have difficulty enjoying this relationship that could serve you well for some time.

Present Moment Living

To live in the present moment means to be fully awake and aware of what is going on outside of us and inside of us as well, as it takes place. Living in this present moment clears away all the debris of the past, and thoughts of the future, allowing us to more fully feel and experience our lives as we live them. We can fully immerse ourselves in our life experiences if we access them through this present moment. If we can live our lives and experience our relationships in each present moment alone, we can then fully feel the depths of love and wisdom they hold.

To make the most of a present-moment healthy relationship:

- Be prepared to let go of a lot of the *expectations* you have of someone else.
- Be willing to live your life in a more creative fashion.
- Be willing to be *flexible* within your present relationship.
- Pay attention to the other person and what their needs are, as well as paying attention to your own.
- Speak up and talk with them about what you think, feel, and want.
- Tell them you would like to hear their feelings, thoughts, and desires.
- Become friends.
- Trust each other.
- Love each other.
- Be together for as long as you possibly can.

What happens when you find you can no longer be present with this other person? Then you need to pull away and take the time necessary to decide for yourself what you want. Be careful when you do this. Tell the other person what your needs are. Ask them if you can possibly take some time out from your relationship. Don't make them panic at the thought you are leaving them, unless you truly realize it's in your heart to do so. Often we just need time away from each other to get clear about what we want. It's alright to give each other this time if you can *trust that the relationship will, in time, tell you the truth of what's meant to be.* Why is it the relationship that's telling the truth and not you? Because we can believe something is over when it's not. Conceivably we have made up our mind to end this relationship only to find later that we are unable to do so.

What do we do when we have ended a relationship and then find this person so present in our lives we feel we are unable to continue without them? It's to our benefit to tell them what we want. What happens if we do this and they decide they don't want to open their hearts to us again? Then we have to respect their choice and do the best we can to take care of ourselves and to get on with our lives.

Potentially you will tell this person you want to be with them again—and they will confess they feel the same way. You then find yourself back in a relationship that you in truth never did leave completely. So what are you going to do? Are you going to continue on as if nothing ever happened, or are both of you going to be called upon to make changes in your lives to accommodate each other? Time will tell.

Be patient with yourself—and with the other person. Love them as you would want to be loved yourself. Treat them the way you would want to be treated. Be kind, loving, and generous with each other. Treat each other as the special human beings you are.

CHAPTER 35

Bringing the Magic
to Our Lives

Relationships are very magical. They can bring you beauty that you will never find anywhere else. It's this magic we so easily become addicted to and find we don't want it to stop. We don't want to lose that loving feeling, the feeling that makes everything else in life glow and sparkle. We want to stay in love for our whole life. What do we do when someone we love doesn't love us? Do we try to hold on to them, or do we let them go? What do we fear we will lose if they leave? *We want to be aware of the fears we have—and to trust ourselves enough to move past these fears.* Once we can begin to do this, the magic will be there in our life, whether someone else is or not.

Ask yourself:

- What do I want and expect from my relationship?
- Do I expect it to be everything that heals my life?
- Do I expect it to bring me great fortunes in gold?

- What do I want and expect? It could be time to release some of these expectations, especially if they depend on someone else giving you what you most need to give yourself. We are coming together with the people we love simply because we love them.
- Why do I think it has to be so much more?
- Am I setting myself up for a major disappointment?
- Do I want to take good care of myself, or do I want to wait until someone else will?
- How long do I think I will have to wait?
- When I do find this person, how much of my responsibility do I think they will be willing to carry, and for how long?

Valuable relationship questions and things to be aware of:

- Look at what you are asking of anyone who comes into your life.
- What do you expect of them?
- Are they willing and able to give it to you? If they can't, what choices are you going to make then as to whether you keep them in your life, or let them go so they can move on with their life?
- What is your priority in life?
- What are you willing to settle for?
- Do you dream of castles in the sky, or are your feet planted firmly on the ground?

Castles in the sky means your expectations of what another can bring to your life may be unrealistic because the other person is only human, after all. This isn't to say that dreams don't come true and love isn't wonderful and grand, but it's important to be aware of what you bring to the relationship because of your *idealized* wants and expectations, as compared to what is really there for you to have and to experience.

Looking at ourselves: 1) What do you want and expect from yourself? 2) What do you have to give this other person? 3) What are you able and willing to share over an extended period of time? Are you compassionate and loving for a while—and then your priorities change and you become lax, taking the other person for granted? What benefit is this? Do you not see the beauty before your eyes? Maybe there isn't enough stimulation and excitement to keep your focus and attention. Again, what do you want? Is there anyone who can truly give it to you, or are you destined to move from one relationship to another in search of that perfect mate who will satisfy all your needs?

It isn't recommended that you stay in a bad relationship because, after all, it's up to you to make it work. What is being asked of you, however, is to look at what you are expecting another person to bring to your life. Why can't you have this without the other person present? Why do you need someone else to provide these things for you? Yes, there are basic needs we all have that the presence of another provides an outlet for, but what about our innermost needs? Who provides for them? Why can't we provide more of these things for ourselves? What are these things? It will benefit us to identify them first.

Some of our basic needs are to trust, love, and support ourselves. When we turn to a relationship, there are times when we want this other person to trust and to love us and to give us the support we need. This is only natural to want from someone with whom you share your life. If, however, we are unable to give this to ourselves, how do we expect another person to give us these feelings; maybe by their presence alone? How long will this last?

Initially, the *infatuation* may seem to be your answer to everything you've always wanted, but what happens when the stage of infatuation passes and you are confronted with real-life situations that demand you stand up for yourself in love and in trust of who you are?

It's essential to consider ourselves when choosing a life partner. Is this someone I can really be happy with over time? If a small inner voice says to you, "I don't think so," pay attention to it. Don't push right on by it to reach out in determination for what your inner instincts are trying to tell you may not be a good match. It can be quite damaging to force ourselves and our relationships. They will come to us in their own time. We may be prepared for them, we may not, but whatever the case we can't force them into being present in our life no matter what we choose to do.

Let go right now. Decide to have the best possible life you can have for yourself whether someone else is in it or not. Work on living your life for yourself and bringing the value you want to yourself. Be kind and patient. Stay detached and trusting of everything that happens to you. Once you can do these things, your ability to attract to yourself someone else of such wholeness will improve day by day.

We can underestimate our own ability to bring magic to our lives. The magic is in us and it's in life itself. Take off your blinders and see the magic that surrounds you every day. Look at the beauty of nature and feel the magic of it in your being. Watch children at play and absorb some of the magic in the way they perceive life and open their arms so easily in love and in trust. Really watch the world around you and the people. People are magical. Each person is unique in their personality and how they choose to live their lives. Feel the magic within yourself. You are magic. You are a miracle of life. Be aware of the miracle of your unique life experience. Be in touch with the peaceful nature of the simple pleasures in your days. There is so much about life to love and to explore. Open your heart and feel all that is present in life for you to experience; that is magic itself.

It's time to honor the beautiful person you are and to know you are fully capable of bringing magic into your own life.

CHAPTER 36
Can a Relationship Bring Us Happiness and Self-Fulfillment?

Be careful who you choose for a life partner. We can think that if we love a person, that's enough. Initially, it may well be, but as time goes on, you will find yourselves growing apart unless you truly have something in common to share. What do you share with your partner? Do you share a common goal for your relationship? If you do, what is it? What do you hope to gain by living with this person, and what do they hope to gain by being in your presence? These are important questions and issues to think about and discuss with each other.

What do we hope to gain from our relationship? Is it happiness and self-fulfillment? If that's our goal, we might want to look deeper within ourselves for what we are trying to make our relationship responsible for. How can a relationship bring us happiness and self-fulfillment? Maybe it can bring us a great deal of love, but what is happiness about? Does it come from the relationship, or does it come from within us? We have to look deeper within ourselves for the answers to this question. It's important to discover what makes us happy and what we are willing to give and to share with another.

How do we expect another person to give us self-fulfillment? Do we think having this other person in our life will suddenly give us the inspiration to live more fully? Initially it may, but in time, you will go back to your old behavior patterns. What do you hope to gain from knowing this person? It's important we look at these questions as well as the answers we have to them. It's of value to learn to understand ourselves better before we can truly share the love we hold inside with another. The better we understand ourselves, the more able we will be to care for and love ourselves. This caring and love we have for ourselves will then run over into the relationship. If we don't have or feel this caring or love for ourselves, what do we expect to be able to share? What do we expect the other person in our life to give us?

It's time we start looking at our relationships in a more realistic manner. To be more realistic requires us to "come down out of the stars." Chances are we have watched too many romantic movies. Yes, it's absolutely wonderful to be in love. The problems begin when we find ourselves "falling out of love." Falling out of love occurs when we are forced to face the human side, the human aspects of the person with whom we are involved. When this occurs, we can do one of two things. We can trust we are being asked to learn from what we are witnessing, or we can reject this person from our heart. How much are we willing to take? How much are we willing to give?

Your love for the special person in your life might be truly tested from time to time. What is it about them that is testing you? Stop and take the time to look at their behavior and what it is about their behavior that challenges you. Do they need to change, or is there something for you to learn and to change within yourself? The work of a relationship requires full commitment and dedication. At times you will want to run away from it all. It can be very painful to witness sides of yourself you don't want anyone, yourself included, to see. Being in a relationship brings to light all the aspects of ourselves we can deny and hide from when we are alone or on our own.

Be willing to do this work. It will bring incredible rewards to your life. You have so much to learn about yourself—and so much of yourself to share with another. It's only when we are willing to do the work of being in a relationship that our relationship can flourish and grow. If you are unwilling to do this work, you might somehow be able to stay with the partner you have chosen, but will you really be sharing much of yourself with them? Naturally, you are most comfortable hiding out because then you won't have to admit to any inconsistencies in your behavior. You won't have to question your worth and your value. Only by doing this work will you realize how truly beautiful and valuable you really are. You will see your beauty reflected back to you in the eyes of your partner. That's a lot to gain from the one you love most.

It's time for us to begin to:

- Be willing to reveal ourselves for our future growth and development.
- Commit ourselves to learning from our relationships with others.
- Not always be in control of everything that occurs and everyone who comes into our life.
- Learn to flow with what takes place around us.
- Learn to bring beauty into our own day.
- Learn to share our innermost self with others.

When we can do all these things, then we will have the life we want to live. We will have a life we treasure. We will have a life that serves many people. It will serve us because we will be at the center of it, but it will also serve those who surround us because we will be able to reach out to them from a place of deep love within our own being, within the depths of our heart.

Happiness and self-fulfillment can be found in a relationship if we can give from our heart. It's only when we can be true to ourselves within the context of a relationship that we can really give from the depths of our heart. All other giving is unimportant if we aren't able to communicate, love, and feel from within ourselves, within our heart. *The heart is the center of our lives.* If our heart is in pain, it's hard to enjoy anything else going on in life. If our heart is healthy and healed, then we have a chance to be in an important, meaningful relationship. When we have a healthy, healed heart, we can love another person without a lot of conditions attached to how we feel about them. When we feel love for ourselves, we can better care for, love, and nurture the person essential to our own existence; ourselves. We do this first for ourselves so our love can move out from within us. When this occurs, everyone benefits.

You can't expect another person to give you your life, to make it happy and fulfilling. Look to yourself for your own happiness. When you have it within yourself, you will be able to share it with another. When you have two people capable of finding happiness within themselves, and also able to share it with others, you have the most profound love of all.

Acknowledgments

A huge thank you to my precious, amazing family and my network of friends who have been so supportive of my writing over the years. A special thank you to my mom who was always there for me. A thank you also to my relationship partners past and present. I've learned so much from all of you as I've analyzed my relationships; what worked and what didn't. I could add some apologies in some areas, but I choose to believe it was and will continue to be a mutual learning experience, filled with compassion and continuing friendships.

Thank you to my soul sister Peggy, Laverne to my Shirley, and our mutual friends who encouraged me to start writing and provided continuing support and inspiration. A thank you to my mentor-friend Colleen who walked this path of publication before me and shares her wisdom with lightness and heart. She also introduced me to the talented women of WOW. A thank you to the WOW (Women on Writing) group who continue to teach and inspire me through their shared experiences, writings and supportive, knowledgeable presences. A thank you to Jim who shared his photography talent and made getting my photo taken not only painless but fun.

With gratitude and hugs to my hospice and home health friends – teammates-volunteers, patients and those family and friends grieving the loss of their loved ones. It was a true gift to meet and be a part of each of your lives. I truly learned so much about being a loving presence in the world. The communications we shared were honest, intimate and upfront. Might we all learn to communicate with each other in this way. Thank you for your trust and friendships. You will forever be in my heart.

A thank you to my Editor Connie Anderson. Your honest appraisal, encouragement and suggestions helped to transform this book.

A thank you to my Editor Nick May who added the final polish to this work of heart.

Thank you to Ann Aubitz at Kirk House Publishers for the powerful cover design and for guiding me through the maze of getting published. Co-creating with you is a joy.

With Gratitude and Love to you all, Carla